SAVING CONTAINER PLANTS

Overwintering Techniques for Keeping Tender Plants Alive Year after Year

---

Alice and Brian McGowan

Storey Publishing

The mission of Storey Publishing is to serve our customers by publishing practical information that encourages personal independence in harmony with the environment.

Edited by and Sarah Guare and Carleen Madigan
Series design by Alethea Morrison
Art direction by Cynthia N. McFarland
Text production by Theresa Wiscovitch

Cover illustration by © Meg Hunt
Interior illustrations by © Beverly Duncan

Indexed by Christine R. Lindemer, Boston Road Communications

Storey Publishing
210 MASS MoCA Way
North Adams, MA 01247
www.storey.com

Printed in the United States by McNaughton & Gunn, Inc.
10 9 8 7 6 5 4 3 2 1

Library of Congress Cataloging-in-Publication Data

McGowan, Brian, 1952–
  Saving container plants / by Brian and Alice McGowan.
    pages cm. — (A Storey basics title)
  Includes bibliographical references and index.
  ISBN 978-1-61212-361-5 (pbk. : alk. paper)
  ISBN 978-1-61212-362-2 (ebook) 1. Container gardening. 2. Perennials. I. McGowan,
    Alice. II. Title. III. Series: Storey basics.
SB418.M325 2014
635.9'86—dc23
                          2014010852

CONTENTS

PART 1

GARDENING WITH TENDERS

Tender perennials are an amazingly adaptable and diverse group of plants.

Because they've arrived in our gardens from so many different corners of the world, tenders introduce wonderful complexities and variations — of texture, bold color, and sheer drama. Caring for them is surprisingly simple when you consider all that they offer the gardener. The diversity of tender perennials lends them to a marvelous variety of uses — these are plants that range from delicate twiners to those that make bold statements, exceeding 10 or 12 feet in height. We suggest that you use your imagination and take your cues from the plants themselves.

WHAT IS A TENDER PERENNIAL?

PUT SIMPLY, A TENDER PERENNIAL IS a plant that, though hardy in its original habitat, will not survive the winter outdoors in the climate of the gardener. Tender perennials in one zone may be perfectly hardy in a different location. But for gardeners in any location other than a truly tropical one, chances are that some plants are tender perennials.

Some tender perennials are, in fact, tropical. But many others come from relatively moderate climates where winters just don't get as cold or, perhaps, as wet as they do where you live. From the temperate climates of the Mediterranean come marvelous gray-leaved plants — like helichrysum and santolina — that require dryness in winter. From New Zealand there are trees and shrubs, even grasses and sedges like *Carex comans*, that make delightful indoor plants. Both South Africa and the South American continent have wonderful plants that simply won't survive outside year-round in other locales, but which (we think you'll agree) can enrich your gardening experience tremendously.

Will tropical and semitropical plants look out of place in your garden? We've spoken with gardeners who worried that this might be the case. We suggest you experiment — you might be surprised. After all, the geographic origins of most hardy perennials are already quite diverse. In our experience, the visual characteristics of plants — their form, texture, and color — are far more important in creating a visually unified and satisfying garden picture.

Location Makes a Difference

The word *tender* suggests that these plants will not survive frost. But many tender perennials tolerate light or sometimes even heavy frosts. They are called tender in a particular place simply because they are unlikely to survive an entire winter in that climate. This distinction may be confusing, but it really needn't be. Even hardy plants respond to freezing temperatures in different ways. Any plant's tolerance of frost and cold is influenced by a variety of factors: hydration, stress, and the plant's recent history. In general, only plants that originate where frost is a common occurrence will withstand it consistently, and even this is not always the case.

....

Perennial vs. Annual

Some gardeners in cold climates think any plant that dies in winter is an annual. The term *annual*, though, refers specifically to a plant that blooms, sets seed, and dies in a single season. Annuals are usually grown from seed. Lettuce poppy (*Papaver somniferum*) and signet marigold (*Tagetes tenuifolia*) are examples of annuals.

To obtain maximum show (bloom) from most annuals, it is essential to deadhead, thereby tricking the plant to create new blooms. Once it has set seed, the plant no longer has a reason to continue blooming. Many annuals will self-sow in your garden; these do, in effect, return each year. This does not make them true perennials, however; they are therefore outside the scope of this book.

In general, perennial plants do not bloom until their second year, and then they live on. Biennials bloom in the second year and then die. Of course, plants don't follow rules very well, and there are exceptions to these definitions, many of which are either short-lived perennials or biennials. Daylilies (*Hemerocallis*) and peonies (*Paeonia*), for example, are perennial plants; sweet William (*Dianthus barbatus*) is a biennial that usually blooms in its second season.

....

Most gardeners have noticed that the ubiquitous hosta, though reliable and quite hardy in a Zone 5 garden, is prone to react extremely to late-spring frosts. In years when these occur, hostas will generally grow an entirely new set of leaves to replace those that succumbed. Although a plant's appearance may be affected for the duration of the season, this doesn't mean that it's not hardy. It's just an indication of the structure of hosta leaves and stems, and shows that once they've begun to grow, hostas are sensitive to frost, despite being hardy to much colder temperatures while in a dormant state. It's also an indication that in their Japanese homeland, frosts rarely occur once the plants have leafed out.

Other plants seem unaffected by cold nights. Some salvias, for instance, will continue as before, generally blooming and carrying on as if nothing has happened. This is a reminder that frost does occur in the desert, where salvias originate, and also that although most tender salvias cannot survive the winter in many colder zones, they are well adapted to life in the spring, summer, and fall in those places.

Origins Are Important

Tender perennial plants come from every corner of the world, and — as the hosta and salvia examples illustrate — it is important to consider a plant's origins in order to understand the best conditions for growing and overwintering it. A desert plant will be happiest in sunny, well-drained conditions of low humidity; one from the Amazon may require both protection from the sun and extra humidity, along with warm temperatures.

Having grown tender plants over the years, we find it fascinating to learn more about their origins. Gardening is one of the most tangible ways there is to gain a deeper appreciation and sense of place through interaction with your very specific plot of land. But it is also a wonderful way to travel imaginatively through both time and space — and to contemplate where in the world a particular plant grew before it arrived in your own garden.

SELECTING WHICH PLANTS TO KEEP

MOST HOUSE INTERIORS tend to be warmer and drier than is ideal for many plants in containers. Are you willing to adjust the thermostat down to 55 or 60°F (13 or 15°C)? Will you remember to water your containers once a week? (Don't forget to provide saucers for all the pots.) These are basic but important questions to consider before you start hauling around those heavy pots.

As tempting as it may be to save everything from the summer patio, be realistic about the storage space you have. A smaller number of plants with more space around them will be easier to keep healthy than a jungle of plants crammed into an area that's too small to accommodate them all.

Your available space for plants is an important factor in determining what will be manageable for you. Assuming that you're considering only those plants that have performed well, begin your selection with ones that would be difficult to replace. A plant might be expensive or relatively rare where you live. Perhaps you grew it from seed that took a long time to germinate or was difficult to obtain. Or maybe the plant was given to you by a close friend or relative and has sentimental value. Everyone has his or her own reasons for wanting to keep a particular plant.

Some plants are so inexpensively and readily available that it doesn't make sense to keep them from one season to another. When such a plant is winter blooming, however, or has particularly attractive foliage and form, it may be worth keeping, especially if it is also easy to care for. Cacti, succulents, durantas, and anisodontea, along with many convolvulus and most kalanchoes, fall into this category.

How you define *low-maintenance* is highly personal and depends quite a bit on the specifics of your space. In a cool sunroom or porch, keeping rosemary happy should be easy. But overwintering the same plant in a warmer, heated living area is guaranteed to be a challenge. In the dry, warm air of most homes,

TWO OF THE MANY fascinating plants you can observe in bloom if you bring them indoors for the winter are *Convolvulus cneorum* and *Pelargonium sidoides*.

it's easy to miss the early signs that this plant needs to be watered, and serious damage may occur before you notice its distress. In a warm space without good air circulation, conditions will also be ripe for the development of mildew or for the proliferation of pests like aphids. By the same token, keeping a brugmansia healthy in a cool, sunny space might not be so difficult — but try it in a warm room and you'll be inviting an infestation of whiteflies. The decision of what to keep for the winter and where to situate it will be informed by many factors. Give each plant some thought well before you need to take action. Remember that when they're happy, plants have a way of growing, and will, in time, occupy more space than they were originally allotted.

WHY GROW TENDERS?

"OH, I GROW ONLY HARDY PLANTS," we've been informed by more than one gardener. And there are certainly arguments to be made for doing this. In general, despite the occasional winter that decimates much of the perennial garden, planting exclusively hardy plants simplifies gardening activities.

But it does limit your options. Even your grandmother probably grew plants in her garden or on her windowsills that were neither annual nor hardy. If she hung her geraniums in the cellar for the winter or kept a sweet-smelling heliotrope in a pot on a windowsill, she was simply overwintering her tender perennial plants. Many gardeners a century ago were familiar with a far greater variety of plants than most are today. One reason is that European and American gardeners of earlier periods were very curious about the many distant places that were still being opened to the eyes of the Western world by plant collectors. Growing the exotic plants that resulted from expeditions to those lands was a tangible way to share in the latest discoveries.

Save Money

In our own consumer culture, plants are viewed as replaceable commodities. Many gardeners simply rely on garden centers and catalogs to supply them with plant products to fill up their gardens each season. These merchandisers produce only those plants that will provide instant and predictable results, regardless of the skills of the gardener. Overwintering tender perennial plants can be a way to save money and to achieve a measure of independence from commercial marketers at the same time. And saving money by not buying the same plants year after year will extend your gardening budget.

Give and Receive

Tender perennials make great gifts for friends and neighbors. Winter bloomers, such as the stunning white-flowered *Convolvulus cneorum*, will remind them of you each winter when their buds open. Or if the summer garden is the plant's moment to shine, your friends will remember your kindness at the height of the seasonal spectacle.

Giving away plants is practical, too. It's common wisdom among professional propagators that you never know when you'll need to ask for a piece of something back. What if you forget to water during a critical time or the power goes off during a prolonged cold spell? If your friend still has the plant you shared with her, she'll be more than happy to return the favor.

Learn New Skills

In the process of learning to grow tender perennials, you'll acquire new propagating skills as you maintain original plants and increase your stock. Saving any kind of plant also increases the amount of control you have over the selection of plants you're growing and of those you will perpetuate for the future. You may have more time to notice your plants when they're indoors, too, and there aren't the million distractions of the summer outdoors. You'll learn more about the varying needs of plants, which change with a specific plant's place in its own life cycle as well as with the season.

THIS HANDSOME BASIL has been trained to a columnar form during its winter storage. Now it adds foliar distinction to the summer garden.

See Plants at Their Best

Saving and storing tender perennials also gives the plants more than one season to mature. Aside from the brevity of the growing season in a place like Zone 5, where we live, many plants just don't reach their full potential in a single season. Some withhold bloom until their second year, and others simply require time to grow large and impressive. Some plants are actually herbaceous in their first season and woody in the next. The young growth of many tender perennial plants — such as salvias, strobilanthes, and durantas — is soft and herbaceous, turning woodier in time. You'll probably learn more about insects, too, as you monitor your plants and keep them healthy. In their second season, they will be ready to create an altogether different and dramatic effect in the garden.

Fill in the Gaps

Many tender plants bloom during those famous gaps in the hardy-perennial bloom cycle. Tender salvias, daturas, and tibouchinas: these and other plants kick in just when most of the perennial border is giving up the ghost. You may be surprised at how much more interesting the August/September garden is when tender perennials are added to your plantings. Their contributions don't necessarily end with the first frost, either. In the chapters that follow, we will show you how to grow and save your favorite plants, and in many cases, how you can continue to enjoy their beauty even through the coldest months of winter.

Who wouldn't want a room full of sweet-smelling flowering plants to enjoy in the dead of winter? No matter where you live, and no matter what your budget, if you choose carefully and consider realistically the conditions of your living space, you'll be pleasantly surprised by the possibilities of your own indoor winter paradise.

PART 2

OVERWINTERING YOUR PLANTS

With all the various ways to overwinter plants, there's sure to be an option that will work for every gardener.

We hope that by now you're convinced that overwintering your tender perennials is worthwhile. You'll save money when you buy plants next year, because you'll already have several to put out into the garden. Many of these plants will have become much larger — ready to be either impressive specimens in the garden or some of the striking elements of your containers.

OVERWINTERING 101

THE KEY TO SUCCESSFULLY BRINGING a plant through the winter indoors is understanding its natural dormancy cycle. Some plants continue to grow during their indoor vacation and thus need a warm, sunny location. Others enter a stage of partial dormancy and are more suited to a spot that's sunny but cool. Some plants go completely dormant and simply need to be properly stored for the winter.

What Kind of Space Do You Have?

Anyone can overwinter tender perennials, but your available facilities will limit and define the possibilities. The options you choose will then depend on how elaborate you want to get and also on your personal preferences.

There are three basic ways to store tender perennials. Each is best suited to certain types of plants. This doesn't mean there is only one way to store each plant, however — just that there may be only one best way.

A SUNNY WINDOWSILL

Some tender perennials — many of them tropical plants like begonias and alternantheras — will be perfectly happy on a sunny east-, west-, or south-facing windowsill. Treat these as you would a houseplant, watering and fertilizing on a regular schedule. If you keep the thermostat between 65 and 70°F (18–21°C), the temperature inside your house will remind these plants of winter in the tropics. This may

A SCENTED GERANIUM and small-leaved coleus share a sunny windowsill.

cause their growth rate to slow slightly, but for the most part, the plants will continue to be in active growth. They will need every bit of sunlight you can supply. Lacking sufficient sun, you might keep them happy with a supplemental source of light, like the fluorescent lights that many gardeners use for vegetable seedlings.

A COOL, BRIGHT SPOT

Another group of tender perennials benefits from a period of relative dormancy in winter, and would be happiest in a very cool but sunny part of your house, such as an unheated porch or a rarely used bedroom. These plants originate in parts of the world that experience dry, cool winters, such as the high elevations of South Africa and parts of the Mediterranean region. They are happiest in a temperature range between 40 and 50°F (4–10°C), accompanied by bright sunlight. The greatest number of tender perennial plants will find these conditions agreeable.

A DARK BASEMENT OR CLOSET

Some plants prefer the dark and will survive the winter in your basement. Most of these can be classified as corms, bulbs, and tubers. Others, such as cannas, like their darkness on the damp side. Still others, like dahlias, will fare better if the conditions are drier. Certain plants from other groups can survive a period of dormancy in the dark almost as well as they might in bright sunny conditions. Some salvias, brugmansias, bananas (*Musa*), lemon verbena (*Aloysia*), *Sinningia*, and *Bouvardia ternifolia* can overwinter in the basement just in their pots.

A subset of the bulbs-and-corms group can be left in the pots they grew in all summer or can be transferred into paper bags. Because they will tolerate warmer temperatures and will not grow until watered, move them into a closet, where conditions will be dark and dry enough to maintain their dormancy. This group includes bessera, *Begonia sutherlandii*, amorphophallus, and certain oxalis.

Overwintering Techniques

In addition to where a plant is stored, it's also important to consider the proper technique for bringing it in for the winter. To find additional overwintering information for particular plants, turn to the Tender Palette on page 75.

Taking Cuttings	page 18	Trim It, Dig It, Spray It	page 22
Storing Tubers	page 30	Storing Dry Corms and Bulbs	page 33
Storing Dormant Woodies	page 37	Storing Plants Outdoors	page 68

SUNNY & WARM

Preferred Temperature: 60 to 70°F (15–21°C)
Possible Locations: south-facing window in warm living area, heated greenhouse or solarium

The first, and perhaps easiest, way to keep plants is to place them inside your living space, where they'll receive the maximum amount of both warmth and light.

This is the best way to store many tropicals, like alocasias, colocasias, and coleus — plants that flourish in seriously warm temperatures (see page 117 for a list of plants that do well stored in warm and sunny locations). These plants would love best to be above 60°F (15°C), in a moist, sunny place — recall the climates they originally come from. It would be safe to say that for this group of plants, the cooler the temperature, the drier the soil conditions should be. In warm temperatures, they'll have much higher requirements for moisture. They will also require extra space to be happy because, under warm and sunny circumstances, the plants will be in active growth, and it's likely that over the course of the winter, they'll increase somewhat in size. It's sometimes difficult to imagine when you look at a relatively small plant, like a seedling or a cutting, how much bigger it will be in just a few months. But even many older plants will increase their dimensions considerably — remember that the winter season will be at least five months long.

If your living space has windows with southern, eastern, or even western exposure, there are many tender perennial plants that you can successfully overwinter in containers. Because of the relative weakness of winter sunlight, southern exposure will give you the most choices, because when they are indoors, the majority of plants benefit from basking in shafts of sunlight.

Succulent plants, which provide a wonderful variety of shapes and textures, are just one group of tender perennials that would enjoy a southern exposure. Most require infrequent watering and make ideal houseplants. Another group that is surprisingly happy in south-facing windows is the begonias. Although southern exposure might be too strong for them in the summer, it seems to be just right when combined with the lower intensity of winter light.

Pots placed in an eastern or western window will necessarily receive more limited light. But the early-morning sun afforded by an eastern windowsill is ideal for some plants, like abutilons and fuchsias. And in winter, even a western exposure, which might be too harsh and hot in summer, can work out well for a collection of begonias or succulents. If you pay attention to the needs

---

Bringing the Sun Indoors

Artificial lighting can be beneficial when storing tender perennial plants in either cool or warm conditions. Even when plants are placed in south-facing windows, the intensity or duration of winter light does not equal that of the spring and summer, and the growth of plants at this time of year is necessarily affected by the difference. Use supplemental fluorescent lighting either to augment the intensity of available light during winter daylight hours or to create additional hours of light in order to extend those shorter winter days.

---

of your plants, and maybe even consider adding supplemental light where necessary, you'll find a suitable spot for a wide variety of tender perennial plants inside your living space.

Just as you benefit from increased humidity in the winter, so will your plants. Although succulents and cacti are not fussy, the majority of other plants will be far happier if the air they grow in is not excessively dry.

Even if you are unable to offer them this relatively convenient and easy winter setting, there are other ways to hold on to your plants from one season to the next. Don't despair, then, if you live in a cold, drafty house, or if your only windows face north. Just keep reading.

Moving in from the Garden

When overwintering plants in a warm, sunny space, consider all the options before bringing the plants indoors. One method is to overwinter cuttings from a plant (see Taking Cuttings, next page). This works especially well with plants that grow quickly and may threaten to monopolize the indoor overwintering space. Softwood cuttings should be taken well before the end of the growing season, so they have time to become established before the low light of winter.

Container-grown plants that are potted up as individual specimens can simply be moved indoors (after being inspected for insect pests). Combination plantings should be dismantled, and each plant should be potted up individually before being taken indoors. Those that have been planted in the ground also need to be potted up (see Trim It, Dig It, Spray It, page 22).

TAKING CUTTINGS

Taking cuttings is an efficient way to keep many different plants in a relatively small amount of space. Larger plants require considerable room to overwinter. They use more water, and also must be pruned and checked for pests more frequently. Overwintering smaller cuttings from a large plant is actually a lower-maintenance alternative.

Turn to page 56 for more information on taking cuttings.

1. Examine the plant carefully, and select longer stems with healthy leaves. The length of your cuttings will depend on the plant, but make sure to choose young growth three to four inches long. Using a sharp implement like a clean razor blade, make a clean cut just below a leaf node.

Make cut just below leaf node.

2. **Strip the lower leaves.** Dip at least half an inch of the stem into rooting hormone.

3. **Make a hole** in the rooting medium with a pencil or chopstick, then stick the cutting into the hole. Water well and label.

4. **Enclose the container** in a plastic bag to maintain a high level of humidity. Place the container in a warm spot, but out of direct sun.

Monitor cuttings frequently, to ensure that the medium is adequately moist.

Check to see if cuttings have rooted after three to four weeks by tugging very gently on them. When sufficient roots have developed, the cutting will not pull up easily out of the rooting medium. At this point, it may be potted up with a well-drained mix and moved into bright light.

Spacing and Temperature

Once the plants have been moved indoors, try to leave plenty of space around each of them. When plants begin to touch one another and their stems start to tangle, take notice. Either move their pots farther apart or prune the plants so that they are smaller. Close physical proximity will usually encourage a plant's new growth to reach upward, resulting in growth that is ungainly and spindly. Lack of air circulation can contribute to the development of diseases like mildew and botrytis, and also enables insect pests to spread among plants. The ideal temperature range for this group of plants is between 60 and 70°F (15–21°C).

Pruning and Grooming

If plants are sharing your living space with you, it's likely that you'll want to groom them occasionally. This can consist of nothing more complicated than cleaning off dead leaves or flowers as they appear. But it can also involve some cosmetic pruning.

A few minutes spent trimming off spindly growth can be quite rewarding. Not only will the plant immediately look better, but its future growth should be affected positively as well. Thoughtful pruning will result in more attractive, compact specimens. Try to cut close to the last leaf node and remember that cuts made at an angle are less obvious than those that are made straight across. Especially as the days get close to spring, do not hesitate to prune off quite a lot. It may look drastic temporarily, but plants really do respond favorably to pruning, and the increase in their vigor will surprise you.

Water and Fertilizer

We've said this before, but it bears repeating: if there is one key to the successful overwintering of tender perennials, it's that it is usually better to under-water rather than to over-water plants. And make sure to let the containers dry out between watering.

At some point during the winter, think about putting some of your plants in the shower. They'll really appreciate the extra humidity, and their leaves will emerge with a much shinier appearance. Alternatively, take a wet cloth or paper towel and wipe larger leaves individually. It is easy to forget how dusty the interiors of our heated houses can get in winter.

As the days begin to lengthen (in late February in Zone 5), start feeding plants lightly with a balanced soluble fertilizer, such as 5-10-10, to encourage growth and flower bud development (see page 62 for more information on fertilizer).

Pests

Aphids, whitefly, and scale are likely to be the major pest issues that occur on plants in these conditions. (For more information, see page 40.)

TRIM IT, DIG IT, SPRAY IT

1. **Cut the plant back to a manageable size.** This means that you'll trim every branch back by at least several inches — it's essential to cut back plants hard at this stage.

2. **Dig up the plant** and shake off the soil clinging to the roots. Then judiciously trim the roots enough to make it possible to fit the plant into the container you've chosen.

3. **Partially fill the pot with soil mix** and set the plant firmly within it. Fill the pot with mix to within half an inch of the rim, gently tamp it down, and water it thoroughly. Check for insects, and spray with horticultural oil.

Keep a watchful eye on your transplant for a week or two after planting. It may require more water and some shade until it has regained its composure.

COOL & BRIGHT

Preferred Temperature: 45 to 55°F (7–13°C)
Possible Locations: unheated sunporch or guest room, cool greenhouse

For the majority of tender perennial plants, the ideal over-wintering situation is a cool space with bright, natural light. This relatively large group of plants includes salvias, phormiums, pelargoniums, fuchsias, most Mediterranean plants, and/or those with gray foliage (see page 118 for a list of plants that do well stored in cool and bright locations). In older or more spacious houses, accommodations for plants like these can often be found in unheated extra rooms or a glassed-in porch or in an attached greenhouse that receives minimal heat or that at least can be kept at a cooler temperature than the rest of the house through the winter. If the space can be maintained above freezing — preferably in the range of 45 to 55°F (7–13°C) — and has abundant natural light, it could be a perfect spot for storing many tender perennials. Don't forget that although these spaces cool off at night, they may require ventilation when the sun heats things up sufficiently in the middle of the day. Temperatures much above 55 or 60°F (13 or 15°C) should be avoided. Particularly as the season moves to late winter, the increased length of daylight combined with the greater strength of the sun will cause temperatures in this type of space to increase; do what you can to keep temperatures cool or your plants will shift into active growth.

The goal, when storing this group of tender perennials, is to prevent them from growing for most of the winter or, alternatively, to let them continue to grow but very slowly. Even though most will retain their leaves, cool conditions — around 45°F (7°C), with bright light — will induce a period of rest that is beneficial. What this means is that they are really pretty low-maintenance for the winter.

Our neighbor and good friend Bobbie Rosenau has successfully stored her salvias and tibouchina for many seasons in just this fashion, using an unheated upstairs bedroom. Of course, if the space is cool and dark, rather than bright, you

Can You Dig It?

If you're going to dig up a plant, it's best to do it as early as possible or when there is a month or so of warm growing conditions left — the roots of the disturbed plant will require at least that long to become reestablished. This is a good time to prune the plant for a number of reasons. By pruning, you will be cutting back on the amount of stem and leaf it has to support, making the transition much easier for the plant. The process of digging will inevitably reduce the size of the plant's roots; the shock of this change will be reduced if its top growth is likewise decreased. It will also diminish the area available for insects to inhabit. Cutting back a plant makes it more manageable to move and care for down the road. It will also encourage compact new growth, which may be advantageous in its more restricted indoor quarters.

could consider adding supplemental light, as many gardeners do when growing their spring seedlings. If the available overwintering space is too warm, the plants will continue to grow. Depending on the plant, this can be undesirable — at the very least, it will complicate matters. When any plant is in active growth rather than a semi-dormant state, it will require more water and more attention in general. If it's something that blooms only once a year, like agapanthus, the warmer temperature could encourage it to bloom while it's indoors, rather than later when it's out in the garden.

Additionally, cool storage conditions will tend to discourage insect problems. Any professional grower will tell you that in the large-scale greenhouse environment, insect problems that are negligible early in winter will suddenly and predictably escalate when conditions warm up and day length increases. Put simply, insects that feed on plants respond favorably to the same conditions that plants do. By discouraging your plants from growing abundantly during their winter storage, then, you will also be minimizing the numbers of insects that feed on them.

Moving in from the Garden

If the plants in question are already growing in containers, check them carefully for insects before bringing them indoors. If you're digging and potting plants, do so well ahead of really cold nights so that they have time to settle into their new containers. Many plants benefit from being cut back hard and sprayed with dormant oil before being taken indoors for the winter. (See Trim It, Dig It, Spray It, page 22, and Can You Dig It?, page 25.)

Spacing and Temperature

One of the most important aspects of spacing is maintaining the ability to actually see how your plants are doing. When conditions are crowded, small plants can easily be lost due to their lack of visibility. Even though cool, bright storage is relatively low maintenance, it's important to keep checking for potential insect and disease issues — they're far easier to control when they're just beginning. Keeping temperatures between 45 and 55°F (7–13°C) is ideal.

Pruning and Grooming

Once inside, unless the plant is becoming unmanageable, it's best to postpone serious grooming projects until the spring. Remove dead leaves and spent flowers from both the plant and its surroundings, but refrain from pruning. Pruning at this time will encourage new growth, which is not always desirable.

Water and Fertilizer

Because the plants are growing very little during this time, they shouldn't be using much water. Feed little, or not at all, between October and most of February. As the days begin to lengthen (in late February in Zone 5), start feeding lightly with a balanced soluble fertilizer, such as 5-10-10, to encourage growth and flower bud development (see page 62 for more information on fertilizer).

Pests

The same potential exists for pest and disease problems no matter where your plants are located, but infestations and outbreaks will be less severe because of the cool temperature. (For more information, see page 40.)

....

No Trimming Needed

A number of tender perennials do not require any pruning. Along with the usual candidates — those with evergreen foliage, such as agaves — there are less obvious ones, such as many perennial grasses. Tender scirpus, carexes, and most of the restio family should never be trimmed by cutting. Instead, pull out the dead leaves periodically to reveal newer growth. Unfortunately, trimming these plants can result in their death.

Another group of plants that don't require much pruning are the slow-growing woody ones, such as punica, sericea, and coprosma. You may want to shape them slightly or thin out weaker growth, but it doesn't make sense to prune these slow-growing plants very substantially; keep it light.

The last group of plants you shouldn't prune before you move them inside is made up of those that bloom in winter, such as bouvardia, ceanothus, citrus, and kalanchoe. You wouldn't want to cut off any developing buds before they have a chance to blossom!

....

DARK & DAMP

Preferred Temperature: 35 to 50°F (2–10°C)
Possible Locations: unheated cellar or garage, crawlspace, cool closet

Older houses often have a cool basement, and this can be handy for storing various kinds of tender perennials (see page 118 for a list of plants that do well stored in dark and damp locations). As long as the pipes don't freeze, your plants shouldn't either. Over the years, we've heard from many of our customers who regularly put their salvias and other tender perennials in the dark cellar, pots and all. Lacking some of the other overwintering options we've discussed, they've found that a dormant period in the basement works surprisingly well for plants that we had assumed required light to survive. We encourage you to experiment with the plants and conditions available to you. The results may surprise you.

Just make sure you remember that the ideal cellar storage for plants and tubers is a *cool* one. Be forewarned that if your cellar is warmed by the furnace and stays at a cozy temperature, this method will probably not work for you. Temperature is critical when it comes to storage in the dark. The ideal range for these plants is between 35 and 50°F (2–10°C). A good rule of thumb is that the darker the storage space, the cooler it should be.

You won't be watering these in the usual way, but it's still a good idea to check on the relative moisture of your storage conditions. Don't allow cannas and other tubers and corms to completely dry out, or their spring viability may be affected. If they seem dry, sprinkle a *little* water on them. Excessive moisture can lead to problems, too. Here, it's key to differentiate between *damp* and *moist*. If the medium within the container is damp enough, it should not dry out all winter; you should still check periodically, however. If the conditions you find are overly wet, open the container to air out a bit to avoid rotting.

STORING TUBERS

1. **Dig up plants** carefully and gently shake off the soil.

2. **Trim** off herbaceous growth, so that just the tuber is left.

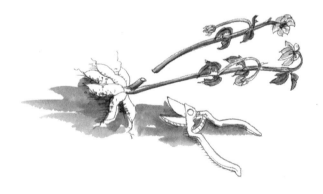

3. **Allow plants to cure** for one or two days in a warm, dry location.

4. **Place tubers** in damp (but not wet) peat moss, inside a storage container that will exclude light, such as a black plastic garbage bag or an old ice chest.

peat moss

5. **Put the container** in a cool, dark place, like a cellar.

Check tubers periodically through the winter and spray lightly with water if needed. Discard any tubers that have rotted.

DARK & DRY

Preferred Temperature: 35 to 50°F (2–10°C)
Possible Locations: unheated cellar or garage, crawlspace, cool closet

Finally, there are those tender perennials that will wait out the winter in the most unpromising conditions. These are mostly corms and tubers, which — like *Bessera elegans* and *Begonia sutherlandii* — can be left in a dry pot inside a dark closet for the duration of the winter (see page 118 for a list of plants that do well stored in dark and dry locations). They will tolerate a warmer temperature than the plants that require dark and damp conditions. As long as they do not come into contact with water, they will simply remain dormant. It is not necessary to wrap them or put them into bags, although if it is more convenient for you, you certainly can. Corms and tubers stored in this way should remain quite dry. This would be an excellent time to separate a few to give away to friends, because bessera, in particular, multiplies like crazy. Just left to sit in a dry pot of soil or emptied into a simple paper bag, these amazing tubers will keep quietly all winter and not demand a bit of attention.

When the days begin to lengthen, bring them back into the light and cautiously begin to water them. Perhaps, like us, you remember those magical paper flowers of childhood that came to splendid three-dimensional life as they gracefully unfolded in an ordinary glass of water. Although bessera won't bloom until later in the summer, upon hydration these little tubers will begin to swell, much like those paper flowers.

STORING DRY CORMS AND BULBS

There are a number of plants that should be kept completely dry during their dormancy. Because they need no attention, these are among the easiest plants to overwinter.

1. **Let the plant go dormant** naturally by slowly cutting back on water.

2. **Dig up corms or tubers** after foliage dies back. Brush off the soil, and trim off all foliage.

3. **Place corms or tubers** in a paper bag or onion sack and hang in a closet or other dark, dry place. Make sure that storage conditions remain dry throughout winter.

THE IMPORTANCE OF TEMPERATURE

IF PLANTS ARE SHARING YOUR LIVING SPACE, the ambient temperature is likely to be determined by what is comfortable for humans, not necessarily by what is best for plants. Examine your plants carefully to determine whether the current overwintering arrangement is working out. Elongated growth and thin, pale foliage can be a sign that conditions are too warm, and that actively growing plants aren't receiving enough sunlight. Perhaps another, cooler area is available that you could move them to, or maybe it's simply time to turn down the thermostat and tell your partner to put on a sweater.

If a plant shows signs of stress from overly cool temperatures, you will have a different set of issues to consider. Does it appear to be losing its leaves? Each plant has its own tolerance for cold, and this threshold is a combination of the actual minimum temperature and the duration of time that temperatures are below what the plant can handle. Such a plant may have wilted, pale leaves that droop despite adequate moisture and fertility. Plants suffering from marginal cold can be difficult to diagnose because their symptoms have involved a long period of exposure. By the time the plant loses its leaves, it might be too late.

Judging whether your plants are in trouble is one of those things you'll learn from experience, and the cause of their distress is not always clear. Just like the symptoms of over-watering and under-watering, sometimes plants lose their leaves and are still fine. The annual behavior cycle of lemon verbena

(*Aloysia triphylla*) is just such a case. Defoliation is part of its normal dormant behavior. After sitting with bare branches the entire winter and looking, well, dead, your lemon verbena plant will revive quickly once the temperatures warm and you begin to water it again. On the other hand, if a coleus loses all its leaves, you probably have cause for serious concern. You could attempt to rejuvenate it by moving the plant to a very warm area — one that does not go below 55°F (13°C) at night and

What to Do in a Frost Emergency

We all have the best intentions of getting to the last garden chores in the final days of summer, and it seems like there's never enough time for everything we need to do. So even if you never had the chance to sit down and consider all your overwintering options, and the first frost came before you had an opportunity to move your favorite pots indoors, it may not be too late to act.

A garage or shed can provide a temporary holding area for tender plants when the weather changes abruptly. Even if your plants get damaged by frost, you can sometimes revive them by pruning them back — for many plants, this is something you were going to do anyway. As long as the temperature hasn't dropped too low, they may survive. If, after a few days, there still seems to be damage to the stem tissue beyond where you cut, the damage may be irreversible. Remember, though, there is an enormous range in minimum temperatures that tender perennials can withstand, and many plants that look terrible now may still bounce back.

stays in the 70s (20–25°C) during the day. If the pot is at all damp, do not water. Just wait and monitor. Times like these are often when we learn the limits of a given winter storage/growing space. If plants are sitting in front of a window that can be opened, make sure that all who might open it on a warm, sunny day understand the minimum-temperature tolerance of your plants! We've heard sad stories from gardeners who've forgotten the window was open when the outside temperature dropped suddenly or the sun moved away. It doesn't take very long at freezing temperatures to do serious damage to some tender perennials.

Plants That Can Be Stored Dormant in the Pot

Aloysia	*Ficus carica*	*Lantana*
Brugmansia	*Iochroma*	*Musa*

STORING DORMANT WOODIES

Many tender woody plants, like fig trees, can simply be stored dormant in their pots. At the end of the summer, wait for a light frost to occur before bringing plants into a dark, cool space.

Many woodies — like fig and lemon verbena — will lose their leaves. In order to encourage dormancy, do not repot the plant. Soil in the pot should be damp but not wet. Be sure to check for any obvious signs of pests as well.

Before overwintering, tender woodies should only be pruned lightly to shape, thin out middle growth, and reduce the plant's overall dimensions (see illustration below, left).

Check the plant periodically during the winter, and water lightly if soil dries out completely (see illustration below, right).

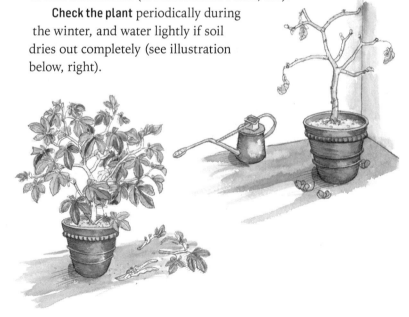

SETTING UP YOUR SITE

THE TIME TO THINK ABOUT all this is in July or early August (in Zone 5), well before the end of the summer. When the weather forecasters predict a hard frost, you'll be much better off if you've already taken care of moving all those pots indoors. And cuttings taken in the dark of an autumn evening are rarely as useful as those you select carefully in broad daylight well before the last minute.

After you make a list of plants you want to save and consider your options for overwintering, it's time to prepare the area you've chosen. Evaluate whether you need to change or augment the existing conditions.

Making Space in the Living Area

If you would like to move plants into your living space, will you need shelves in front of a window to accommodate all of them? Do you have enough trays or dishes to put under all their containers? If you have many small containers, consider setting them on large trays constructed of either sheet metal or plastic. This will enable you to water them easily, as long as you remember to place plants with similar moisture conditions in the same tray. The water that collects in the tray will also contribute to the ambient humidity, which is desirable in heated spaces. For that matter, how dry is the heat in your living area? This may be a good time to purchase a humidifier if you don't already have one. Tropical plants prefer conditions that are warm, but also quite humid.

When setting up a cool, bright location in which to overwinter plants, make sure that temperatures can be modified. You should be able to prevent freezing or alternatively keep it from overheating. Some form of ventilation is necessary for sunny days. Is additional light required? Even though the space is cool, there should be good light.

Down Below

Perhaps you've decided to use part of your basement for plant storage. Although an unheated basement is generally better for this purpose than a heated one, you could also adapt part of the existing space within a heated basement area. One method is to create a small, separate room adjacent to one of the basement windows. Section off the area with some type of wall — the more insulated, the better — and then open the window just a crack, and you have a workable storage area.

If you don't require access to the basement through the bulkhead door, you can turn it into an excellent storage area for bulbs, tubers, and semi-dormant plants (those that have died back for the winter). First, thoroughly insulate any surface that is directly exposed to outside temperatures, especially the metal doors. The ideal temperature range for this type of storage is between 35 and 40°F (2–4°C).

PREVENTING PEST PROBLEMS

EXPERIENCE WILL TEACH YOU which plants are insect bait. Those prone to infestations may not be worth the time and trouble. Look carefully at each plant — if, like us, you're over the age of 40, use your reading glasses to make certain that the plant is clean. Concentrate particularly on a plant's growing points, the undersides of its leaves, and in the leaf axils. When insect populations are building up on a plant, these are the locations where their presence will be most obvious. If there are problems, take the time to deal with them now, before you move the plant into an enclosed space, where any insects will quickly multiply and spread to other plants. Plan on making a regular inspection of your plants — once a week would not be too often.

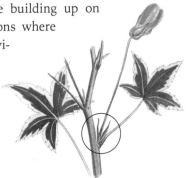

APHIDS TEND TO CONGREGATE in the leaf axil of a plant — the point where the leaf meets the main stem.

Spraying with Oil

We have had good success controlling most insect problems with either horticultural oils (such as Sunspray) or insecticidal soaps. Look for summer oil, a type of horticultural oil that can be applied to actively growing plants. It's critical to follow the product directions and to test a small amount first; these substances can still harm some plants. These materials work by smothering insects but are nontoxic to people and animals, which makes them an excellent choice for plants in your living space. To minimize the amount that you inhale, we recommend that you wear a mask while spraying them.

If you do find an infestation, spray at least twice before moving the plant indoors. This is simply a good preventive measure — even if you have well-trained eyes, it's easy to miss a small number of tiny insects.

Remember that applications will be most effective if you recognize a problem and treat it in its early stages. Later, it will be more difficult to conquer, as many a gardener has discovered to her dismay. To avoid damaging your plants, don't apply dormant oil when plants are stressed for moisture. It's also important to avoid periods of high humidity, because the oil must dry quickly after it has been applied.

SPRAYING PLANTS with summer oil before overwintering them is a good way to avoid pest infestations indoors.

SPECIFIC PESTS AND DISEASES

THE FIRST AND MOST IMPORTANT STEP in coping with pests and diseases is correct identification. It is amazing how rarely most gardeners bother to do this before attempting a solution. Each type requires its own treatment, so take the time to figure out exactly who or what your unwelcome guest is.

Diseases

The most common diseases that pose problems for the indoor gardener are mildew, botrytis, damping-off, and root rot. It is possible to prevent their occurrence by employing a combination of temperature control, air circulation, correct watering, and adequate sanitation. Although they are in widespread use within the greenhouse industry, fungicides are something we have never used in the 20 years we've grown greenhouse crops.

Botrytis is also referred to as "gray mold," which is a pretty good description of its appearance. Its most common manifestation is on dead leaves and flowers, which explains why removing these from a plant and taking them away — otherwise referred to as sanitation — is important. Because the spores of this mold require moist

BOTRYTIS CAN ANNOUNCE its presence through the appearance of brown and gray zones on live plant tissue.

conditions for a period of 8 to 12 hours with temperatures between 55 and 65°F (13–18°C), sufficient air circulation is another key to its prevention and control. The mold may actually be present on dead and decaying plant parts and not bother healthy, living tissue if conditions are not optimal for its growth.

Damping-off and **root rot** are caused by a variety of fungi. Both cause plants to wilt, droop, and eventually die. In the case of damping-off, you will see a specific weakening point in a plant's stem as the disease advances, and once it establishes a toehold, it will travel from plant to plant quickly, particularly among seedlings. Evidence of root rot is clearest below the soil. Affected roots will discolor and have a foul odor. The plants themselves will lose vigor and may wilt even when the soil is moist.

You should be able to avoid both of these diseases by using a well-drained soil mix and watering properly. Water only when the pots are dry, and then water thoroughly. Be especially careful during periods of cool, cloudy weather. Plants use considerably less water under these conditions, making it much easier to over-water at these times.

A PLANT WITH ROOT ROT will emit a foul odor. A dark root color is sometimes a tip-off as well.

Once either disease is present, you should dramatically cut back on watering, and also consider changing your soil mix. In the case of root rot, it might also be helpful to trim the affected roots. After cutting, let them dry until they form callus tissue on the cut areas. None of these approaches can guarantee saving your plant, however.

Recent research indicates that the use of compost in soil mixes may offer particular benefits when it comes to preventing and managing soil-disease problems. Compost is generally rich in beneficial bacteria and fungi that take up space and feed on nutrients — the same nutrients that disease-causing microbes might otherwise make use of. Their presence makes it more difficult for disease organisms to become established (remember that nature abhors a vacuum). Much about the microbial and chemical activity of soils is still unknown to us — soil is a mysterious and highly complex environment, and exciting information concerning the interaction of plants and soil microbes continues to be discovered.

Powdery mildew differs from these other fungi in that it does not require water for infection to occur. Water may actually kill its spores and inhibit the growth of this disease. Powdery mildew has the appearance of a fine white powder, and although not all plants succumb to it, those that do generally have a specific type of powdery mildew to which only they are susceptible. For example, the powdery mildew that affects lilac bushes will not spread to the rest of a garden. Likewise, the powdery mildew that covers your summer phlox will remain confined to the phlox plants you unfortunately included in the border.

Warm temperatures and high humidity are both prerequisites for its growth — on both indoor and outdoor plants — but the temperature range varies with the specific mildew.

POWDERY MILDEW is particularly common on rosemary plants when wintered indoors.

Among plants often wintered indoors, rosemary is infamous for attracting powdery mildew. We have found that keeping the plant in a cool space with bright light is key to the avoidance of powdery mildew — and also results in a happy, healthy plant. Another way to control powdery mildew is by selecting individual plants within vulnerable groups that seem to have better resistance than is usual. This is the type of characteristic that professional breeders watch and select for. On plants where powdery mildew has been discovered, repeated applications of summer oil, or baking soda mixed with water, may reduce or stop its spread.

Insect Pests

Aphids are probably the most common problem gardeners encounter when they bring plants indoors. In the garden, aphids are part of the larger ecosystem. If the environment is diverse, and if you have not used insecticides, you should have a resident population of insect predators and parasites that will keep the aphid population under control. When you move plants indoors, however, some aphids will surely travel with them.

Aphids are small, slow-moving, soft-bodied insects that tend to appear in groups on the undersides of leaves and on the tips of plants. They also have a brief stage in their life cycle when they can fly. Curling leaves on a plant may be a sign that you have them. Individual aphids vary quite a bit in size and color, depending on the species. Often their body color seems selected to match the host plant — shades of green are common — but it's also possible that their color is affected by the juices of the plant on which they are feeding. We have always found the bright orange aphids that usually situate on butterfly weed (*Asclepias*) fascinating in this regard. In warm conditions, aphids reproduce very quickly, causing their populations to increase dramatically.

Cutting back the plants before moving them inside will help to reduce populations. Spraying with summer oil after cutting the plants is also effective. If your storage conditions are cool enough, you probably won't have an overwhelming problem. The most challenging period will be in spring, when the temperature warms up. If aphids are

CURLING LEAVES may be a sign that your plant is harboring aphids.

Using Oil and Soap

In our experience, insecticidal soap is somewhat less effective than horticultural oil, but it may be safer for use in some cases because of the adverse reactions certain plants — like succulents — can have to horticultural oil. If you're trying to control insects without using more toxic materials, insecticidal soaps may be useful.

Because insecticidal soap is a relatively benign product, thorough and adequate coverage is critical, as is the repetition of applications. Mix the soap according to the instructions on the label and spray in a fine mist onto the foliage and stems. Spray plants at least twice to ensure adequate coverage.

on your plants, keep a close eye on them and consider spot treating with insecticidal soap or summer oil.

If your plants are spending the winter in a greenhouse, consider using beneficial insects to control aphid infestations. Over the years, we have developed management plans for our greenhouses that use insect predators and parasites almost exclusively.

Fungus gnats are small, mosquito-like gnats that lay their eggs in soil, which is where the small worms hatch. Although the adult gnats are bothersome, it is the larvae that do the serious damage, feeding on roots and stems near the soil. Their presence can also enable the introduction of decay organisms.

We've found that a combination of careful watering and reasonable sanitation practices is the best way to avoid fungus gnats. The grubs feed on decaying plant debris, so it makes sense to eliminate their food; then they'll be less inclined to stop by. Applying a coarse, dry mulch on top of the soil, such as calcined clay, can also help to prevent infestations. Mulching containers establishes a dry surface on top of the soil; this creates an environment that is inhospitable to fungus gnats.

Once a population of fungus gnats (and their larvae) is established, there are a few options for eliminating them. Start simply by allowing the soil to dry out completely, and water only sparingly afterward. If this isn't successful, you might try repotting the plant with fresh potting mix. (Remember that prebagged mixes may not have adequate drainage and may therefore have the potential to become breeding grounds for fungus gnats. You might be better off making your own well-drained mix.) As a last resort for tackling a widespread or particularly stubborn infestation, you might treat the plant with beneficial nematodes (which will eat the gnat larvae) or drench the soil with a dilute dose of *Bacillus thuringiensus* (Bt).

AN ESTABLISHED POPULATION OF FUNGUS GNATS (and their larvae) can be eliminated by doing any of the following: letting the soil dry out thoroughly, watering the plant with a Bt solution, or simply repotting with fresh mix.

INDIVIDUAL MITES are hard to spot with the naked eye, but their webbing is quite apparent.

Predatory mites (generally available through mail-order companies; see page 120) may also be effective.

Mites are so small that if you are of a certain age, you may not be able to focus on the individuals with your naked eye. You can generally recognize their presence, however, by a telltale mottling of the affected leaves. In severe infestations, white webbing will also be present. If you look at mites with a magnifying lens, they resemble tiny spiders, and come in a wide range of colors, from bright red (this tends to be a winter coloration) to very pale yellow and tan.

Horticultural oil works well on mite infestations after they have been discovered, but continued monitoring is essential and repeat treatments may be necessary. There are also many species of predator mites that feed on the mites that attack plants. They work well in greenhouse situations and are worth trying even inside your house if you have a lot of plants in combination with a mite problem.

SCALE AND MEALY BUGS are small, sucking insects that, for the most part, sit stationary on the plant.

Scale and **mealy bugs** are small sucking insects that spend most of their time stationary on the plant, although there is a youthful "crawler" stage when they move around a bit. Some scales are "armored," which means they have a hard shell; others are soft-shelled. Mealy bugs are covered with a white, wax-like material.

Insecticidal soaps and horticultural oil are effective controls, but your plants will probably require several treatments. Scale and mealy bugs can be particularly stubborn; after spraying, you'll want to wipe the plants with a cloth to ensure that you remove all the insects.

Thrips are small, soft-bodied insects that are longer (about $\frac{1}{16}$ inch) than they are wide. Their color varies: brown, yellow, and black are most common. When the weather is warm, they

THRIPS FEED on the undersides of leaves, creating a characteristic appearance.

will crawl rapidly. You can see them with the naked eye if your vision is good, but they are easiest to recognize by the damage they inflict. They feed primarily on plant buds, both flower and shoots, but also enjoy the undersides of leaves. These feeding patterns result in a characteristic appearance that should alert you to the presence of thrips on a plant. The leaves they feed on will appear streaked with white and the buds will be deformed.

Some control is possible by spraying with dormant oil. In our experience, though, for severe infestations, the most long-lasting control is the introduction of predator mites (*Amblyseius cucmeris*).

Whiteflies are very small insects that appear whitish in color. The adult flies lay eggs on plants, from which nymphs hatch, and these nymphs feed on the plant. We have never had a problem with whiteflies, in part because they prefer warm temperatures between 70 and 75°F (21–24°C), and we kept the plants in our greenhouses at much cooler temperatures during the winter. But we were also very lucky, and Brian has always quarantined new plants for observation before introducing them into the larger

WHITEFLIES are a fairly challenging problem to control; if you notice them on a plant, you may want to reconsider your decision to overwinter it.

Tips for Avoiding Indoor Pests

- *Prune back and carefully check plants for insects before bringing them indoors, and quarantine new purchases for at least two weeks before putting them in close quarters with other plants.*
- *Be vigilant: conduct weekly inspections.*
- *Keep temperatures on the cool side, and water plants only when soil is dry.*
- *Place blue or yellow sticky traps among the plants in order to monitor whitefly and thrips populations.*
- *Be open to the idea that you may not be able to save plants that are frequently problematic in your storage conditions. Plants susceptible to whiteflies, for instance, will be challenging to store on a warm windowsill.*

greenhouse environment. This is a recommended practice; it is surprising how often plants are commercially distributed with problems like whitefly in evidence.

If you are keeping tenders in the warm part of your house, you may run into problems with certain plants. Whiteflies seem to have a particular attraction for specific groups of plants, such as the Solanaceae and the Verbenaceae. If you notice them on a plant, reconsider your decision to keep that particular plant, because whiteflies are a fairly challenging problem to control. Oil will kill the nymphs and may smother the eggs, but you must continue to monitor and spray again if necessary. Some growers effectively use beneficial insects to control whiteflies; if you have an infestation, we encourage you to learn more about this possibility.

SPRING: THE TRANSITION

WHEN SPRING WEATHER ARRIVES, you can begin to move plants back outside, as the temperature permits. Most of the hardier plants, such as salvias, agaves, abutilon, agapanthus, haloragis, and lavender, can go out fairly early (April in Zone 5). The tropical plants, like cannas, dahlias, begonias, abelmoschus, alternanthera, and *Hamelia patens* should be kept indoors longer. Keep an eye on the weather. Any extreme conditions could set back tender herbaceous growth.

Potting and Pruning

If you plan to keep the plant in a container or to use it as an element in a combination container planting, this is an excellent time for a transition. Before the plant enters this period of increased growth, it is important to make sure that all the conditions within your control are optimal. At the very least, this means giving the plant new soil; chances are that most of the nutrients you added to last summer's mix have been depleted over the season and the structure of the soil has been compromised.

When repotting a plant, take it out of its old pot and refresh the roots, either by teasing smaller root systems with your fingers or with a cultivator. In the case of larger, tougher roots, cut through them in a few strategic spots with your pruning shears.

Now is also the best time to prune plants — before they begin spring growth. Select weak and damaged growth for pruning. If the plant is a woody one, prune to open up the center. If your tender perennial was growing under less-than-ideal conditions, it's a good idea to prune this weak growth in order to promote better form and structure. Don't be afraid of cutting back; remember that pruning promotes new growth. At the same time, don't cut too much from woody plants — after all, you've stored them all winter in order to give you this much more substantial plant.

Prune weak growth

After trimming, place the plant in a container of freshly mixed potting soil and tamp it in. Make sure the soil line is at the same height on the plant's stem as it was previously. At the same time, leave at least half an inch of space between the soil and the upper edge of the pot to facilitate watering. If you are combining it with other plants in a single container, try to imagine

SOME OVERWINTERED PLANTS become leggy because of low light conditions indoors. Prune this weak growth to promote better form.

(and then allow enough space for) each plant's eventual spread. Consider, too, the growth habit of the plant and the orientation of the pot.

POTTING UP BULBS AND CORMS
This is a good time to bring out any bulbs or corms you stored for the winter and pot them up in the containers you have chosen for their summer lives. Discard any bulbs or corms that have become rotten or have questionable spots. Plant them root-side down in fresh potting mix and water them in. Place them in a sunny place that's not too warm; they'll grow best in a relatively cool location until you can move them outside.

POTTING UP PUPS
A few plants, among them agaves, alocasias, aloes, bromeliads, and musas, produce basal offsets, or miniature new plants. These are commonly referred to as "pups" and might be defined as new plants that form on underground shoots or rhizomes of their mother plants. If you have a mature plant that is surrounded by a ring of babies, it may be time to liberate them from the central plant and to pot them up individually.

Spring is probably the best time to do this, but if it is more convenient for you to do it in fall, there's no reason you can't. If the plant is a prickly one, wear gloves to protect

TO PREVENT THE SPREAD of disease, it's important to pot up only solid, blemish-free corms.

should still look good. The plant's nonflowering shoots are the best ones to gather for cuttings.

softwood

hardwood

SOFTWOOD is more pliable than hardwood and easier to break off the stem.

Using sharp tools will enable you to be precise in your cuts. Brian prefers a pair of Felco pruners that he uses only for cuttings, so that the blades always remain sharp. But a small paring knife or even a good pair of scissors can do the job, too. And be prepared to sharpen any of these when they lose their edge.

In the past, gardeners simply took cuttings, stuck them in a glass of water or in a jar, and kept them on an east-facing windowsill. This has worked well for many plants and many gardeners over the years. Alternatively, however, you can use a purchased rooting hormone. Although it is possible to encourage the growth of roots on new cuttings without it, the application of rooting hormone will improve your chances of success, especially with plants that are more difficult to root, such as those that have woody stems.

If you decide to use rooting hormone, mix it with water if it requires dilution, and put the solution into a fairly small container, so that you can dip the cut stems easily into either the liquid or powder. Rooting hormone is available in different strengths — those for use with woody plants are generally of greater strength than those needed for herbaceous tropical plants. Some require dilution to achieve the desired strength. After you've used a batch of rooting hormone, it is best to discard it.

After dipping the stem in rooting hormone, stick it into some perlite, where it can remain until it is well rooted. You can use small pots or flats to hold the perlite, depending on the space you have set aside for this project. Tamp down the perlite into the container. Use a pencil or a chopstick to create vertical spaces that are narrower than the diameter of your cuttings before sticking them in.

Once you have stuck in all the cuttings, water the container well and place it in a warm spot out of direct sunlight. Placing the cuttings on a low-energy heating mat (rubber-coated and specifically designed for propagation) will encourage rooting. Keep the perlite moist; enclosing the plant and its container in a plastic bag will help maintain a high level of humidity. This will decrease the amount of moisture lost through the leaves and stem tissues of the plant while it is busy creating roots. Once the cuttings are planted, they will grow roots most quickly where conditions are fairly warm. When propagating big-leaved plants, like larger coleus, it may be beneficial to cut the leaves in half. This approach is not necessary for smaller-leaved plants such as rosemary and lavender.

CUTTINGS from large-leaved plants should be cut in half to mitigate moisture loss.

Be patient, and take careful note of the cutting's appearance. Once it has rooted, it will begin to grow more vigorously — an excellent visual clue. After two or three weeks, give the plant a gentle tug to determine whether it has developed roots. Once the roots have developed, pot the cutting in a 3½- to 4-inch container and dispose of the plastic bag. Resist the urge to overpot. A small plant in a large pot will result in soil that stays wet too long. The plant will grow faster and be healthier in a pot that dries out periodically. After root formation, most plants benefit from being moved to a cooler location. Remember not to let them dry out at this vulnerable stage.

LEAF CUTTINGS

Begonias are an excellent example of a plant best propagated by leaf cuttings. Cut a leaf into sections, with the edge of the leaf forming the top of the cutting. The base of the cutting should be longer than the top and include one of the leaf's larger veins. One of the best rooting mediums to use is perlite, because of its excellent capacity for drainage. Using a knife or other slender tool, make a narrow opening in the perlite that corresponds to the length of the cutting's base. Dip the base of the leaf cutting into rooting hormone, then stick it vertically into the perlite. Water well and enclose in a plastic bag. Monitor the humidity — you shouldn't have a great deal of condensation inside the bag, because begonias are prone to rot. Keep cuttings out of direct sunlight; an eastern window is ideal.

SUCCULENT CUTTINGS
root in flats of perlite.

Many succulents can be propagated from their leaves. With these water-storing plants, it is not necessary to cut a leaf into sections. Simply place the base of the leaf into the perlite. Eucomis is another plant that can be propagated from leaf cuttings. Cut the long, straplike leaves of eucomis into 1- or 1½-inch sections, making sure you keep the basal ends of the cuttings oriented similarly. Slice the perlite with a knife and insert the basal end of each cutting into it.

Water

Because their rate of growth has increased dramatically in the spring, you should expect that your plants will require substantially more water than they did during the winter. Especially on warm, sunny days, they will go through a surprising amount of water. It's still good to let the containers dry out between watering, however.

Do yourself a favor and buy a watering wand for your garden hose. A "water-breaker" that fits on the end of the extension makes it even more useful. This simple gadget is a large nozzle with numerous holes that facilitate the delivery of copious amounts of water to pots without washing away their soil.

Fertilizer

Longer daylight hours will encourage plants to increase their rate of growth, but additional fertility will influence its quality. As the days grow longer, begin adding some nutrients either to the water you give the plant or to the soil in which it is planted.

SOLUBLE FERTILIZER

One of the great conveniences of soluble fertilizers is that they can be used each time you water or at weekly intervals. Follow the recommendations on the package, and keep records of what works well for various plants under specific conditions. The amount you use will depend on the formulation — a higher percentage of N, P, and K (nitrogen, phosphorus, and potassium) will require a smaller amount to be efficacious. For example, 20-20-20 delivers twice as much fertilizer as the same amount of 10-10-10.

If you use a hose for watering, especially when the plants are outdoors, consider investing in one of the readily available devices that inject concentrated fertilizer solution into the hose. The strength of the dosage can be controlled either by the mechanism itself or by the concentration of the fertilizer solution in your bucket. These injection devices range from fairly expensive and complex models to simple siphons that are very affordable. Designed for professional use, the more expensive injection systems do provide greater precision and are adjustable, but their cost is probably prohibitive for most gardeners. The siphon models should be completely adequate.

Another piece of equipment that is worth considering when fertilizer is injected into the water supply is a back-flow preventer. In the event that there is a momentary loss of water pressure, this will prevent fertilizer from draining back into the water source.

SLOW-RELEASE FERTILIZER

Many gardeners and professionals prefer slow-release fertilizers, in part because they eliminate the necessity for repeated applications. These fertilizers release to the plant relatively small doses of balanced nutrients through a permeable membrane. Simply sprinkle some on top of the soil; the granules will release small amounts with each watering. Alternatively, incorporate the fertilizer granules into the soil mix when it is first being prepared.

....

Fertilizing Tips

Remember that small amounts applied frequently are more valuable to a plant than large amounts provided less often. You can always adjust the fertilizer dose and add more, if this seems necessary.

Synthetic fertilizers are a form of salt, and in excess, they will harm the roots of plants. Once a plant has been burned, it will take some time to recover. Keeping records is particularly useful here as you discover what works and what doesn't work in caring for your plants.

We've found that including a dilute concentration with every watering is an easy way to avoid mistakes.

....

Like many other fertilizers, these are available in a variety of concentrations. Once again, follow the directions supplied by the manufacturer. And bear in mind that though the effects of these fertilizers can last for a year, they are temperature dependent — this means that the cooler the ambient temperature, the more slowly nutrients will be released. They are also available in a range of time durations, so some will continue to perform over a longer period than others.

SLOW-RELEASE FERTIL-IZER is sprinkled directly on top of the soil.

ORGANIC OPTIONS

From a chemical standpoint, the main difference between organic fertilizers and their synthetic counterparts is that the synthetic fertilizer is more readily available to a plant. The immediate availability of synthetic fertilizers is a positive factor, but the downside is that it is much easier to overfeed plants with synthetic fertilizer, and excessive amounts can also be harmful to soil microbes. The N, P, and K of an organic fertilizer are not as readily available to plants, and the concentrations tend to be lower, which means you'll have to apply greater quantities in order to deliver sufficient nutrients to them. But its slower release can be beneficial, both to plants and to soil microbes.

These days, any well-supplied farm and garden center stocks an overwhelming selection of fertilizers. Take time to read the labels, and then keep notes on what works well for you. When they are successful, try to stay with the same formulations and similar products. Remember, too, that not all types of plants require the same level of fertility. Many tropical plants — because they grow quickly, have large leaves, and bear abundant flowers — will need more fertility than those from the Mediterranean region, which have developed characteristics that conserve moisture and nutrients under their native harsh growing conditions.

What Does That Yellow Leaf Mean?

The yellowing of a plant's lower leaves may be a sign that it is not getting sufficient nitrogen. This can be confusing, however, because the same symptoms might be caused by either too much or not enough water. Generally speaking, if overwatering or underwatering is your problem, there should be yellow leaves distributed over an entire plant. This is where there is no substitute for being in tune with your plants — older leaves will also naturally yellow and fall as they age. Particularly when you first move many plants indoors, they are likely to spend some time losing leaves. This is a natural response to both the shock of transition and the ending of the outdoor growing season. Try to resist over-watering when this happens; it may be that all a plant needs is some time to adjust.

Pest Issues

Just as the longer days of spring encourage plants to grow, this increase in day length is also an important trigger for insect populations. Be vigilant and carefully monitor insect presence on your plants — catching any infestation early is your best defense. Most insect problems, as long as they are not too severe, will improve automatically when a plant moves outside. Cooler temperatures and the availability of other host species will usually diminish the population on any one plant. This may constitute a significant enough relief that a plant will be able to rebound and repel further infestations.

If you are fortunate enough to have a greenhouse or a large sunroom dedicated to plants, you may want to consider the use of beneficial insects. This approach is not necessarily an easy one, but it will result in an environment for both you and your plants that is free of toxic chemicals.

Once your plants move outdoors, the world of naturally occurring, beneficial insect parasites and predators will become a factor. If you don't use toxic sprays, your garden should already contain a healthy population of these. Remember that a few aphids here and there is a sign that your insect predators won't go hungry!

Hardening Off

As weather permits, help your plants acclimate to outside conditions gradually. Even if they have spent all winter in a southern window, the much greater amount of sunlight outside will be a severe shock if plants move out all of a sudden. Similarly, after months spent in the shelter of your house, they are unprepared for the buffeting winds and fluctuations of air temperature that are a normal part of any spring day outside. This is why most gardeners engage in a process commonly referred to as hardening off.

Hardening off usually involves moving a plant, or selectively protecting it from outdoor conditions, in order to prepare it for full-time life outside. It generally takes place over a week

Tender 911

Accidents happen, and every once in a while, tender plants will be hit by frost. Here are a few tips to help an affected plant recover.

- *Don't do anything rash. Give a plant time — wait and watch.*
- *Don't over-water. Keep it in the shade. If temperatures remain cool, move it to a warmer location.*
- *After a few days, if the leaves do not recover, trim them off.*
- *If the growing points of the plant are damaged, prune back branches or stems to healthy tissue.*
- *Keep the plant in a warm location and water normally (avoiding over-watering) until it begins to put out new growth.*

or two. Ideally, the weather will be cooperative and give you daytime temperatures above 50°F (10°C) with relatively little wind. Some rain is fine as long as it's warm and not accompanied by high winds.

The most important thing is not to leave the plants unattended to fend for themselves at night, when the temperatures are much lower. In the evening, either move the plants back under some cover or, if they are too large to move easily, have some substantial covers ready to arrange over them. After three to five days of this process, plants will generally be ready to handle the outdoors on their own. But remain vigilant about the weather — if temperatures dip considerably, you may need to take precautions.

STORING PLANTS OUTDOORS

SOME PLANTS DON'T FIT into the basic three categories we have outlined. These plants tend to originate in regions with winter conditions that are slightly less severe than yours. They're often big — perhaps a bit too large to store indoors practically. They may also benefit from a period of dormancy, so that storage in a place that is both cooler and darker than indoors is ideal. (Many of these plants could also be stored in cool and bright conditions if the environment is cool *enough* to encourage dormancy, so that light is no longer such an essential component and water becomes less critical.) Such plants can be good candidates for storage in protected outdoor or semi-outdoor locations.

Plants That Can Be Stored Outdoors

bay laurel (*Laurus nobilis*)

Angel's trumpet
  (*Brugmansia* species)

fig trees (*Ficus carica*)

olive trees (*Olea europaea*)

peach trees (*Prunus persica*)

New Zealand flax
  (*Phormium tenax*)

gunnera
  (*Gunnera manicata*)

rosemary
  (*Rosmarinus officinalis*)

Add other plants within two hardiness zones of yours that prefer winters drier than your own. If your indoor space is adequate, most of these could also be stored in cool and bright conditions.

What Sort of Outdoor Storage?

Pits and trenches. The most common way to store plants outdoors is in some kind of pit or trench. You will probably want to lay the plant in its container on its side, so dig a fairly deep trench — one that more than allows for the plant's width and is also a bit longer than the plant's height. Pack insulating material — such as leaves, newspaper (shredded paper makes for easier packing), Reemay, or burlap — into the pit and add more insulation around the plants themselves. All of the materials you use to insulate the plant should breathe — moisture-trapping plastics are an invitation to diseases. This process is necessarily one of trial and error, as no two pit locations are precisely the same, and no two winters are either.

Unheated garages and sheds. These are most useful when they are insulated — just like conditions below the ground. Insulation reduces temperature fluctuations, which can stress your plants. You are far more likely to have success over-wintering your plants in an insulated structure that is attached to a heated building than you are in one that lacks insulation and stands alone. Everything you can do to ensure consistent temperatures will help, including wrapping individual plants with paper and/or burlap. For a reliable back-up in unusually cold weather, you could consider adding a space-heater on a thermostat.

Some Specific Recommendations

Bay laurel. This has a tendency to dry out when stored in standard indoor conditions, but a more pertinent note is that with time it can grow quite large, outgrowing most indoor spaces. This makes it a good candidate for pit or out-building storage.

Figs. In the more northern parts of Europe, it is common practice for gardeners to plant figs against south-facing walls not only to protect them from winter winds but also to retain heat during the growing season. In the United States, gardeners as far north as Columbus, Ohio — where an urban gardener made use of a south-facing brick wall and wrapped the tree with leaf-filled paper bags — have had success with this method.

And there is always the classic outdoor pit favored by many Italian-American émigrés of the last century. To do this, dig a trench that is wider and longer than the fig tree and in a well-drained area. You may want to prune some of the larger branches as suggested below. Set the pot or root-ball in the trench and lay the entire tree on its side. Fill in the trench with about 6 inches of soil and top with another 6 inches of fairly porous mulch material, such as leaves.

Figs can also be left in a pot and overwintered in an unheated garage. Some garages are better suited to this use than others; ideally, the temperature in the garage should not go below 15°F (-9°C). Allow the plant to become dormant and lose its leaves in the fall before moving it into the garage.

Yet another approach is to keep the fig tree in the ground and wrap it up. As the leaves begin dropping in late fall, remove some of the oldest and thickest branches. This makes the tree easier to wrap because the remaining stems are thinner and therefore more pliable. Using a thick cord, gather the stems into a vertical bundle, beginning at the bottom and winding the cord up in a tight spiral. Stuff burlap into any gaps at the base, wrap more around the bundled stems, and secure the wrapping with string. Wind a waterproof covering of roofing felt from bottom to top. Cover the hole at the top with an upturned bucket and tie it on, allowing space for ventilation. We know someone who lives in Zone 6 and has successfully used this approach for 12 years on a fig that is near a sidewalk in a suburban setting. Some gardeners suggest putting a space heater on a thermostat inside the wrapping. Your success will obviously depend upon your location.

Gunnera. Perhaps the most famous gunnera (giant rhubarb) in cultivation living outside its comfort zone is at Frank Cabot's garden, Stonecrop, in Cold Spring, New York. Gardeners there built a large insulated box with an insulated lid to keep their magnificent gunnera alive over the winter. An electric light bulb contributes warmth to this prickly plant.

New Zealand flax. The main challenge to storing New Zealand flax (phormium) is that the plants dislike wet winter conditions. So if you can store them in a cool to cold place that is dry, such as an insulated outbuilding or garage, they have a much better chance of survival. Needless to say, New Zealand flax plants are generally large, so it's nice to get them out somewhere where space is not at a premium. Stored plants should not be subjected to temperatures that go below freezing.

A Note about Microclimates

When evaluating the winter-hardiness of plants, remember that microclimates can make a huge difference in your success. Not only the orientation of your planting, but the soil type, moisture, and prevailing winds will all affect winter-hardiness. Your plants' proximity to heat-storing structures, such as masonry walls, patios, and, most especially, heated buildings can influence the outcome. This means that in the right location, you may not need to dig up your plant and move it to a special storage place. It might be best just to leave it in the spot where you planted it.

Peach trees. If you live someplace where growing peaches outdoors is a risky proposition but you really want tree-ripened peaches, you could try growing a peach tree in a large pot and wheeling it into the garage for the winter. We know someone who did this. That's not to say we would do it, but it all depends on how fresh you like your peaches.

Rosemary. This plant is notoriously difficult to overwinter in living spaces and really is much happier where conditions are cooler than for human comfort. You might reduce the chance of mildew developing — another curse of rosemary — by not watering it. While we favor storing the plants in unheated structures, such as insulated garages and outbuildings, it's also possible that rosemary would survive winter insulated by a well-dug pit. Since rosemary should be hardy to –5°F (–20°C), you have some latitude with this plant, unless you garden very far north.

Other overwintering possibilities include choosing exceptionally hardy selections that will survive in the ground outdoors, and/or planting them in unusually protected sites, such as walled or sunken gardens, or near buildings or patios.

Salvias. Salvias are a colorful and diverse group that like winters to be dry and cool. With adequate protection, downright cold might work, too. While we prefer to store them in a cold, semi-outdoor space, such as a garage or shed, it's possible that you could insulate them and successfully store them in a trench. The hardier salvias are probably your best bets for overwintering — we would begin with *S. guaranitica*, which sometimes overwinters with no protection in Zone 7.

Summer-blooming bulbs and/or tubers. These can be left in situ, in the ground, when the location is sufficiently protected by a masonry wall, sidewalk, patio, or other landscape element that affects soil temperature. In the right location, and over the right winter, tender tubers like acidanthera and mirabilis often survive and re-sprout in the spring. Experiment!

PART 3

THE TENDER PALETTE

The first step toward success with tenders is selecting the right plant for the kind of over wintering space you have.

Much of our experience with the storage of tender perennials has taken place inside our nursery's greenhouses, but we've also stored them in our home — both in our living space and in the unfinished basement. We've also learned a tremendous amount about the storage of tender perennials from conversations with our customers, who have devised some ingenious methods for holding on to their favorite plants through the decidedly unfavorable conditions of the average New England winter.

QUICK TIPS FOR OVERWINTERING

EVERY GARDENER FACES SOMEWHAT DIFFERENT growing and storage conditions. Your own conditions are a unique combination of light, temperature extremes, and the type of potting mix you've used. Because of this, it's difficult to give general instructions that apply to everyone in every situation. We firmly believe that a gardener can learn much of what he or she needs to know about how to care for a plant simply by observation. To avoid problems, we recommend that you check on your plant frequently throughout the winter, even if it's tucked away in the basement or an unused part of the house.

To prune or not to prune? This is a question that continues to perplex gardeners of every stripe. Throughout this section of the book, we've indicated when a plant can be cut back hard, either before it's been brought indoors or during the winter. Except for a few exceptions (see page 28), most plants will tolerate being cut back. Plants that grow very quickly can be cut back drastically.

Watering through the winter. A plant's water requirements are affected by its age, size, and whether or not it's actively growing. When plants grow outside, the humidity, light, and temperature all affect how much water they use — these conditions determine how much moisture evaporates before it reaches the plant's roots. When a plant is grown indoors, the amount of water it needs to receive is dependent on these same conditions. Whether you keep your living space very warm, heat with a woodstove (which dries out the air), or live in a house that's built into a hillside makes a difference in your indoor ambient humidity and thus affects how often you need to water your plants while they're sharing your home. Developing a sense of how to give plants what they need is going to keep you in much better stead than if you were following the arbitrary directions of someone who isn't familiar with your surroundings.

Inserting your finger into the soil to test for moisture — or the lack of it — is a perfectly good way to assess whether a plant needs to be watered. You can often gauge dryness just by looking at the color of the soil at the top of the pot. If you study your plants, you'll also observe subtle changes in leaf color when they become dry. You'll also notice when they begin to wilt. Slight wilting is not necessarily a bad thing. It is far better for the plant than keeping the soil saturated with water — the resulting lack of air space in the soil may lead to disease.

Feed me? In general, fertilizing plants is appropriate when they are in a period of vigorous growth, and most plants that are being overwintered indoors should need little or no fertilizing through the winter. No matter what kind of fertilizer you use, when you pot up a plant, you may find it helpful to label the plant with information about when it was potted, what amendments you added, and whether you incorporated a slow-release fertilizer.

PLANT BY PLANT

Abutilon (flowering maple, parlor maple)
Hardy to at least 35°F (2°C)

OVERWINTERING. Cool, sunny window. Abutilons bloom profusely in winter and should be fertilized lightly. They can get scraggly, especially in less than full-sun conditions, so don't hesitate to prune leggy branches back hard. (See Cool & Bright on page 24.)

PROPAGATING. Cuttings can be taken at most times of the year.

COMMON PEST PROBLEMS. Aphids are fond of abutilons. (See Specific Pests and Diseases, page 42.)

Acalypha (Jacob's coat)
Hardy to at least 45°F (7°C)

OVERWINTERING. Warm and sunny (see page 14). Acalyphas are slow-growing, so prune gently if you want to shape your plant.

PROPAGATING. Cuttings should be taken during periods of active growth but before the plant blooms.

COMMON PEST PROBLEMS. None.

Agapanthus africanus (lily of the Nile)
Hardy to at least 25°F (-4°C)

OVERWINTERING. Cool, with bright light (see page 24). The cooler the conditions, the later agapanthus will bloom. When stored at 40°F (4°C), in Zone 5 it is possible to delay bloom until June or July.

PROPAGATING. Division. This method requires considerable exertion, but is also a necessity as the plant matures. Agapanthus does have a preference for being pot-bound — tight confines encourage it to bloom. You can also grow it from seed, but this will be a much lengthier process.

COMMON PEST PROBLEMS. Scale. (See Specific Pests and Diseases, page 42.)

Agave (century plant)
Hardiness varies; most are hardy to at least 25°F (-4°C)

OVERWINTERING. Agaves are equally happy in cool or warm conditions, as long as they receive plenty of light. Some gardeners prune off the sharp tips of threatening leaves to make them more companionable housemates. (See Sunny & Warm, page 14, and Cool & Bright, page 24.)

PROPAGATING. Division of the pups that eventually surround the mother rosette. If your species agave blooms, you can also collect seed, but growing them this way is a slow process.

COMMON PEST PROBLEMS. Occasionally, scale can pose a problem indoors, especially when conditions are very warm. (See Specific Pests and Diseases, page 42.)

Aloe (aloe)
Most species hardy to at least 35°F (2°C)

OVERWINTERING. Room temperature and bright light. Cool and bright conditions work well, too. (See Sunny & Warm, page 14, and Cool & Bright, page 24.)

PROPAGATING. Aloes are easy and quick to grow. Many species do not *reproduce* particularly quickly, however. Be patient and eventually you'll have offsets you can divide.

COMMON PEST PROBLEMS. None.

Alonsoa (mask flower)
Hardy to at least 45°F (7°C)

OVERWINTERING. Cool and bright (see page 24). This rangey grower benefits from frequent and fairly hard pruning.

PROPAGATING. Both cuttings and seeds. Cuttings are best taken in late winter.

COMMON PEST PROBLEMS. None.

Aloysia triphylla (lemon verbena)
Hardy to at least 25°F (-4°C)

OVERWINTERING. Cool and bright, although some gardeners have had luck storing dormant lemon verbena in a dark, cool basement. Prune back to live growth in the spring. (See Cool & Bright, page 24.)

PROPAGATING. Cuttings.

COMMON PEST PROBLEMS. One of the best reasons to let lemon verbena go dormant in winter is to avoid insect infestations — particularly those of spider mites and whiteflies. This is a good example of how dormancy can benefit some plants. When they're hard up, aphids can also become interested in lemon verbena. (See Specific Pests and Diseases, page 42.)

Alternanthera (alternanthera, Joseph's coat, joyweed)
Hardy to at least 25°F (-4°C)

OVERWINTERING. Warm and sunny (see page 14).

PROPAGATING. Cuttings.

COMMON PEST PROBLEMS. None.

Amarcrinum (amarcrinum)

Hardy to at least 25°F (-4°C)

OVERWINTERING. Cool and bright (see page 24).

PROPAGATING. Will produce bulblets that are easily separated from the parent plant and potted up.

COMMON PEST PROBLEMS. None.

Amorphophallus (devil's tongue, voodoo lily)

Corm is hardy to at least 45°F (7°C)

OVERWINTERING. Store corms where it is dark and dry, either closeted in their pot or placed in a paper bag. Try not to eat them all — they are edible and quite tasty. (See Dark & Dry, page 32.)

PROPAGATING. Amorphophallus corms will produce numerous offsets. It takes three to four years for offsets to reach blooming size.

COMMON PEST PROBLEMS. None.

Anagallis (pimpernel)

Hardy to at least 15°F (-9°C)

OVERWINTERING. Cool and bright (see page 24). This plant's scraggly habit is much improved by occasional hard pruning.

PROPAGATING. Roots easily from cuttings taken in late winter; also can be grown from seed.

COMMON PEST PROBLEMS. None.

Angelonia angustifolia (summer snapdragon)
Hardy to at least 35°F (2°C)

OVERWINTERING. Cool and bright (see page 24). Cut back hard at end of summer.

PROPAGATING. Cuttings.

COMMON PEST PROBLEMS. None.

Anigozanthos (kangaroo paw)
Hardy to at least 35°F (2°C)

OVERWINTERING. Cool and bright (see page 24). It is especially important to water only sparingly in winter. In summer, when they are in active growth, they require much more water.

PROPAGATING. We have usually grown our kangaroo paws from seed; however, it is also possible to divide plants with especially desirable characteristics.

COMMON PEST PROBLEMS. In the garden, kangaroo paws attract slugs. Slugs may be discouraged by copper barriers, but the most reliable way to eradicate them is through cultural practices that encourage air circulation and good soil drainage.

Anisodontea hypomadara (African mallow)
Hardy to at least 35°F (2°C)

OVERWINTERING. Cool and bright conditions (see page 24) should ensure winter bloom. Shear the plant, or do more fine-tuned deadheading on a regular basis. They respond well to pruning.

PROPAGATING. Cuttings.

COMMON PEST PROBLEMS. Aphids. (See Specific Pests and Diseases, page 42.)

Arctotis hybrida (African daisy)

Hardy to at least 35°F (2°C)

OVERWINTERING. Cool and bright (see page 24).

PROPAGATING. Cuttings.

COMMON PEST PROBLEMS. Aphids. (See Specific Pests and Diseases, page 42.)

Argyranthemum (marguerite, Paris daisy)

Hardy to at least 35°F (2°C)

OVERWINTERING. Cool and bright (see page 24). Cut back in late fall to promote winter bloom.

PROPAGATING. Cuttings.

COMMON PEST PROBLEMS. Aphids. (See Specific Pests and Diseases, page 42.)

Ballota (ballota)

Hardy to at least 25°F (-4°C)

OVERWINTERING. Cool and bright (see page 24).

PROPAGATING. Cuttings.

COMMON PEST PROBLEMS. None.

Begonia (begonia)

Hardy to at least 45°F (7°C)

OVERWINTERING. Either warm and sunny or cool and bright (see pages 14 and 24); begonias are an adaptable group of plants.

PROPAGATING. Leaf or stem cuttings.

COMMON PEST PROBLEMS. None.

Bessera elegans (bessera, coral drops)
Hardy to at least 35°F (2°C)

OVERWINTERING. Either in the pot and placed in a dark place or simply inside a paper bag. (See Dark & Dry, page 32.)

PROPAGATING. From the many cormlets the mother plant produces.

COMMON PEST PROBLEMS. None.

Bouvardia (bouvardia)
Hardy to at least 35°F (2°C)

OVERWINTERING. Cool and bright (see page 24).

PROPAGATING. Root cuttings.

COMMON PEST PROBLEMS. None.

Brachyglottis (brachyglottis)
Hardy to at least 25°F (-4°C)

OVERWINTERING. Cool and bright (see page 24).

PROPAGATING. Cuttings.

COMMON PEST PROBLEMS. None.

Brugmansia (angel's trumpet, brugmansia)
Hardy to at least 35°F (2°C)

OVERWINTERING. Brugmansias should be stored in their pots for the winter in cool and bright conditions. Prune to maintain a manageable plant. (See Cool & Bright, page 24.)

PROPAGATING. Cuttings taken before flower-bud initiation.

COMMON PEST PROBLEMS. Whitefly. (See Specific Pests and Diseases, page 42.)

Canna (canna)

Hardy to at least 25°F (-4°C)

OVERWINTERING. Dark, cool, and moist — though make sure rhizomes stay above freezing. Dig up rhizomes before frost hits, and store in a tightly closed plastic trash bag or ice chest (see page 31). (See Dark & Damp, page 29.)

PROPAGATING. It's easy to propagate these productive plants. Simply separate the rhizomes according to size and the number of containers you want to fill. Keep in mind that even a fairly small rhizome will provide quite a show.

COMMON PEST PROBLEMS. None.

Capsicum (capsicum, pepper)

Hardy to at least 25°F (-4°C)

OVERWINTERING. Cool and bright (see page 24). You can continue harvesting peppers through the winter, too. Sometimes an older plant will benefit from hard pruning.

PROPAGATING. From seed or cuttings.

COMMON PEST PROBLEMS. Aphids. (See Specific Pests and Diseases, page 42.)

Carex (carex, sedge)

Hardiness varies; most are hardy to at least 5°F (-15°C)

OVERWINTERING. Cool and bright (see page 24). Do not cut back. Simply remove old foliage by pulling out individual blades.

PROPAGATING. Division or from seed.

COMMON PEST PROBLEMS. None.

Ceratostigma wilmottianum (ceratostigma, Chinese plumbago)

Hardy to at least 15°F (-9°C)

OVERWINTERING. Cool and bright (see page 24). Given these conditions, ceratostigma will bloom happily most of the winter.

PROPAGATING. Cuttings.

COMMON PEST PROBLEMS. Aphids sometimes like this plant. (See Specific Pests and Diseases, page 42.)

Cestrum (cestrum, jessamine)

Hardy to at least 35°F (2°C)

OVERWINTERING. Cool and bright (see page 24). Cestrum has a tendency to get a bit rangy — don't hesitate to prune fairly hard to shape the plant in the fall, but avoid removing the flower buds.

PROPAGATING. Cultivars are best propagated from cuttings, but the species may be propagated from seed.

COMMON PEST PROBLEMS. None.

Chondropetalum tectorum (restio)

Hardy to at least 20°F (-7°C)

OVERWINTERING. Cool, bright, and dry. Do not prune — simply remove old leaves by pulling them off the plant. (See Cool & Bright, page 24.)

PROPAGATING. Seeds or division. Because chondropetalum occurs in fire communities in its native South African habitat, germination of the seed requires exposure to smoke.

COMMON PEST PROBLEMS. None.

Citrus (citrus)

Hardiness varies

OVERWINTERING. Cool and bright (see page 24).

PROPAGATING. Cuttings.

COMMON PEST PROBLEMS. Scale. (See Specific Pests and Diseases, page 42.)

Colocasia (colocasia, elephant's ear, taro)

Hardy to at least 45°F (7°C)

OVERWINTERING. Either warm and sunny or dormant and cool in a plastic trash bag or ice chest (see page 31). (See Sunny & Warm, page 14, and Dark & Damp, page 29.)

PROPAGATING. Offsets from the tubers.

COMMON PEST PROBLEMS. Aphids. (See Specific Pests and Diseases, page 42.)

Convolvulus (bindweed)

Most species hardy to at least 45°F (7°C)

OVERWINTERING. Cool and bright (see page 24). It's critical to keep these plants dry; let them dry out well between waterings.

PROPAGATING. Cuttings

COMMON PEST PROBLEMS. None.

Coprosma (coprosma)

Hardy to at least 45°F (7°C)

OVERWINTERING. Cool and bright (see page 24).

PROPAGATING. Cuttings.

COMMON PEST PROBLEMS. None.

Cordyline (cabbage tree)
Hardy to at least 45°F (7°C)

> OVERWINTERING. Cool and bright (see page 24).
> PROPAGATING. Seed or cuttings.
> COMMON PEST PROBLEMS. None.

Cosmos atrosanguineus (chocolate cosmos)
Hardy to at least 25°F (-4°C)

> OVERWINTERING. Unearth the tubers after frost has affected the tops. Store in slightly moist peat moss, as you would dahlias. Alternatively, leave in the pot over the winter and do not water. (See Dark & Damp, page 29.)
> PROPAGATING. The tubers will produce offsets or you can take cuttings early in spring.
> COMMON PEST PROBLEMS. None.

Cotyledon (cotyledon)
Hardy to at least 45°F (7°C)

> OVERWINTERING. Cool and bright (see page 24). Water sparingly.
> PROPAGATING. Cuttings taken from nonflowering plants.
> COMMON PEST PROBLEMS. None.

Crassula (crassula)
Hardy to at least 35°F (2°C)

> OVERWINTERING. Cool and bright or at room temperature in your living space. (See Sunny & Warm, page 14, and Cool & Bright, page 24.)

PROPAGATING. Cuttings. Choose young growth and stick into a well-drained mix. Crassulas require remarkably little water, and fragments that drop into the soil beneath an established plant will often root on their own.

COMMON PEST PROBLEMS. None.

Crocosmia (crocosmia, montbretia)
Hardy to 10°F (-12°C)

OVERWINTERING. Dark and dry (see page 32).

PROPAGATING. Propagate by planting new cormlets or from seed.

COMMON PEST PROBLEMS. None.

Cuphea (cigar plant)
Hardy to at least 25°F (-4°C)

OVERWINTERING. Cool and bright (see page 24). Prune back plants by half at the end of the summer.

PROPAGATING. Cuttings.

COMMON PEST PROBLEMS. Aphids. (See Specific Pests and Diseases, page 42.)

Dahlia (dahlia)
Hardy to at least 25°F (-4°C)

OVERWINTERING. Dig up tubers and store in damp peat moss for the winter. Alternatively, if they were growing in a container, leave them in the pot and place in the dark. Keep the soil slightly damp. (See Dark & Damp, page 29.)

PROPAGATING. Collection and division of tubers.

COMMON PEST PROBLEMS. None.

Datura (thorn apple)

Hardiness varies

OVERWINTERING. Cool and bright (see page 24). Daturas do tend to grow a bit rangy; feel free to prune back to a desirable shape and size.

PROPAGATING. Seeds.

COMMON PEST PROBLEMS. None.

Dianella caerulea (flax lily)

Hardy to at least 35°F (2°C)

OVERWINTERING. Cool and bright (see page 24). Avoid pruning just before bloom.

PROPAGATING. Division.

COMMON PEST PROBLEMS. None.

Diascia (twinspur)

Hardy to at least 25°F (-4°C)

OVERWINTERING. Cool and bright (see page 24). Prune hard in late summer, and repeat as necessary.

PROPAGATING. Cuttings, although the species grows easily from seed.

COMMON PEST PROBLEMS. Aphids. (See Specific Pests and Diseases, page 42.)

Dichondra argentea (dichondra)

Hardy to at least 45°F (7°C)

OVERWINTERING. Cool and bright (see page 24).

PROPAGATING. Sow fresh seed in the fall. Dichondra can also be grown from cuttings, although plants will take some time to develop.

COMMON PEST PROBLEMS. None.

Dicliptera suberecta (dicliptera, jacobinia, justicia)

Hardy to at least 45°F (7°C)

OVERWINTERING. Cool and bright (see page 24). Prune as desired to maintain a compact shape.

PROPAGATING. Cuttings.

COMMON PEST PROBLEMS. None.

Echeveria (echeveria)

Hardy to at least 25°F (-4°C)

OVERWINTERING. In your living space, as long as there is adequate light; otherwise, cool and bright. (See Sunny & Warm, page 14, and Cool & Bright, page 24.)

PROPAGATING. Division of offsets.

COMMON PEST PROBLEMS. None.

Erysimum (wallflower)

Hardy to at least 5°F (-15°C)

OVERWINTERING. Cool and bright (see page 24). Trim off spent flowers, and prune to maintain a compact shape.

PROPAGATING. Cuttings.

COMMON PEST PROBLEMS. None.

Eucomis (pineapple lily)

Hardy to at least 25 °F (-4°C)

OVERWINTERING. Cool and bright (see page 24). Water sparingly.

PROPAGATING. Seeds; leaf cuttings.

COMMON PEST PROBLEMS. None.

Felicia amelloides (kingfisher daisy, blue marguerite)

Hardy to at least 45°F (7°C)

OVERWINTERING. Cool and bright (see page 24).

PROPAGATING. Cuttings.

COMMON PEST PROBLEMS. None.

Ficus carica (common fig)

Hardy to at least 5°F (-15°C)

OVERWINTERING. Cool and bright (see page 24). For specific fig overwintering techniques, see page 70.

PROPAGATING. Layering is the favored method, although cuttings can also be taken from mature wood. To layer, select 8- to 12-inch shoots and bury them so that only a few nodes are above the soil surface. Hardwood cuttings can also be taken after the tree has lost its leaves — preferably no later than the end of December. With either method, developing sufficient roots on fig cuttings is not a quick process — they may become established by the end of the following year.

COMMON PEST PROBLEMS. Scale. See page 50 for suggestions on how to cope with an infestation.

Fuchsia (fuchsia, lady's eardrops)
Most hardy to at least 45°F (7°C)

OVERWINTERING. Cool and bright (see page 24). Because fuchsias need more water than do many other plants, we recommend that you store them individually. Be careful not to let them dry out completely, but don't allow them to become waterlogged either. They may have difficulty if planted in containers that are too large. Generally speaking, pruning fuchsias is a good idea. If plants become lanky, cut them back hard. Of course, any trimming will probably result in the loss of some flower buds, but the plant will also respond with greater vigor.

PROPAGATING. Cuttings taken in late winter or early spring.

COMMON PEST PROBLEMS. Botrytis is fond of fuchsia, and the paler-flowered forms seem to be most susceptible. In the winter months, many fuchsias are also prone to rust, which can be discouraged by the removal and disposal of infected leaves. Aphids and whiteflies can also pose a problem. (See Specific Pests and Diseases, page 42.)

Gardenia (gardenia)

Hardy to at least 25°F (-4°C)

OVERWINTERING. Cool and bright (see page 24). The humidity supplied by a greenhouse or conservatory environment is best. If you lack these special conditions, mist frequently and keep the humidity as high as you can. A humidifier may help considerably. If your plant is getting rangy, prune it back hard.

PROPAGATING. Cuttings.

COMMON PEST PROBLEMS. Red spider mites. Keeping the soil dry in winter and feeding regularly during warmer weather may help prevent infestations. (See Specific Pests and Diseases, page 42.)

Gladiolus (gladiolus)

Most species are hardy to at least 30°F (-1°C)

OVERWINTERING. Wait for early frosts to kill foliage in the fall, then cut the stems a few inches above the corms. Dig them up, shake off soil, and sort by cultivar. Allow corms to cure in an airy, warm space for about three weeks. Then separate the older, spent corms that bloomed this season from the smaller new corms, discarding the old ones. Store corms in well-ventilated, dark, dry, and cool conditions. (See Dark & Dry, page 32.)

PROPAGATING. The very smallest corms, known as "cormels," may be saved and grown on in subsequent seasons.

COMMON PEST PROBLEMS. Glads are susceptible to a number of pest and disease problems. To minimize these, discard any mushy or unsound corms. Thrips are a major pest issue. Storage temperatures between 35 and 40°F (2–4°C) may reduce the chances of thrip damage. As an added precaution, the corms can be dipped briefly in 160°F (71°C) water, then dried thoroughly before storage. Practice crop rotation when planting them out, choosing a different location each season. If foliage appears streaked or stunted, they may be infected by a virus and should be discarded.

Gunnera manicata (giant rhubarb, gunnera)
Hardy to at least 25°F (-4°C)

OVERWINTERING. A controversial question. Some gardeners have successfully overwintered *Gunnera manicata* in the ground in Zone 5, but this requires fairly elaborate coverings, as well as electric lightbulbs and insulation to keep the plant crown warm, not to mention the cooperation of Mother Nature. For most gardeners in colder climates, growing it in a pot, which is brought inside during the winter, is probably the most reliable approach. If temperatures are sufficiently cold — around 35°F (2°C) — store gunnera in the dark. Otherwise, keep your gunnera in cool and bright conditions. (See Cool & Bright, page 24, and Dark & Damp, page 29.)

PROPAGATING. Seeds.

COMMON PEST PROBLEMS. No insect pests or diseases have dared to bother our gunneras, but persistent wind can cause damage to the leaves, especially when a plant first moves outdoors. For this reason, make sure to maintain adequate moisture for your plant, especially during such transitions, and choose a moving day that isn't terribly windy. Alternatively, create a protective structure or shield to help your gunnera adjust to the move.

Gynura aurantiaca (velvet plant)
Hardy to at least 40°F (4°C)

OVERWINTERING. Warm and bright (see page 14).

PROPAGATING. Cuttings.

COMMON PEST PROBLEMS. None.

Haloragis erecta (haloragis)
Hardy to at least 45°F (7°C)

OVERWINTERING. Cool and bright (see page 24). Occasional pruning will keep this plant more compact.

PROPAGATING. Cuttings or seeds.

COMMON PEST PROBLEMS. None.

Hamelia patens (firebush, hamelia)
Hardy to at least 45°F (7°C)

OVERWINTERING. Cool and bright (see page 24). This plant likes regular watering. Frequent pruning may be necessary to keep it happy in a pot.

PROPAGATING. Cuttings.

COMMON PEST PROBLEMS. None.

Haworthia (haworthia)
Hardy to at least 35°F (2°C)

OVERWINTERING. In your living space, but if light conditions are not adequate, cool and bright is also fine. (See Sunny & Warm, page 14, and Cool & Bright, page 24.)

PROPAGATING. Division of offset rosettes.

COMMON PEST PROBLEMS. None

Hebe (hebe)

Hardy to at least 25°F (-4°C)

OVERWINTERING. Cool and bright (see page 24).

PROPAGATING. The cultivars should be propagated by cuttings.

COMMON PEST PROBLEMS. Aphids. (See Specific Pests and Diseases, page 42.)

Heliotropium arborescens (cherry pie, heliotrope)

Hardy to at least 33°F (1°C)

OVERWINTERING. Cool and bright (see page 24). Heliotrope's growth will slow considerably in cool temperatures, but it will continue to bloom. You may want to prune back straggly growth.

PROPAGATING. Cuttings.

COMMON PEST PROBLEMS. Aphids seem to find these as sweet as humans do. (See Specific Pests and Diseases, page 42.)

Hibiscus (Chinese hibiscus, mallow)

Most hardy to at least 45°F (7°C)

OVERWINTERING. *Hibiscus rosa-sinensis* prefers warm, sunny conditions; *H. acetosella* can tolerate much cooler temperatures. (See Sunny & Warm, page 14, and Cool & Bright, page 24.)

PROPAGATING. Cuttings.

COMMON PEST PROBLEMS. Aphids, whitefly. (See Specific Pests and Diseases, page 42.)

Iochroma (iochroma)

Hardy to at least 35°F (2°C)

OVERWINTERING. Cool and bright (see page 24). Prune hard to soften the plant's naturally lanky habit.

PROPAGATING. Cuttings.

COMMON PEST PROBLEMS. None.

Ipomoea (moonflower, morning glory, sweet potato vine)

Hardiness varies, but few are hardy beyond 5°F (-15°C)

OVERWINTERING. When keeping any vining or twining plant in a temporary confined space, it is desirable to limit its growth. For this reason, keep ipomoeas in as cool an environment as possible to discourage winter growth. They do best on the dry side. Alternatively, cut back the vines and store the tubers in dark, somewhat damp conditions. (See Cool & Bright, page 24, and Dark & Damp, page 29.)

PROPAGATING. Some types, such as *Ipomoea indica*, can be propagated only by cuttings; others start as tubers — *I. batatas*, for example. These are also delicious to eat, so make sure you save a few to plant in your summer containers. All of the *I. tricolor* cultivars are easily started from seed.

COMMON PEST PROBLEMS. The only insect to bother our ipomoeas is a distinctive one — the sweet potato leaf beetle. This beetle has a rectangular, iridescent body, and generally arrives as soon as plants are set outside in the spring. It punctures the foliage with multiple holes but doesn't seem to hurt the plants seriously. Indoors under cool temperatures, red spider mites may also be a problem. (See Specific Pests and Diseases, page 42.)

Jasminum (jasmine, jessamine)

Hardiness varies

OVERWINTERING. Cool and bright (see page 24).

PROPAGATING. Cuttings.

COMMON PEST PROBLEMS. Whiteflies. (See Specific Pests and Diseases, page 42.)

Juncus (rush)

Hardiness varies; most are hardy to at least 15°F (-9°C)

OVERWINTERING. Cool, bright, and dry. (See Cool & Bright, page 24.)

PROPAGATING. Divide; in the case of the species, start from seed.

COMMON PEST PROBLEMS. None.

Kalanchoe (kalanchoe)

Hardiness varies

OVERWINTERING. Cool or room temperature with sun. (See Sunny & Warm, page 14, and Cool & Bright, page 24.)

PROPAGATING. Cuttings.

COMMON PEST PROBLEMS. None.

Kniphofia (kniphofia, red hot poker)

Hardy to at least 5°F (-15°C)

OVERWINTERING. Cool, bright, and dry. (See Cool & Bright, page 24.)

PROPAGATING. Species are grown easily from seed, the hybrids should be propagated from divisions.

COMMON PEST PROBLEMS. None.

Lantana (lantana, shrub verbena)
Hardy to at least 45°F (7°C)

OVERWINTERING. Sunny and warm or dormant in the pot (see page 36). (See Sunny & Warm, page 14.)

PROPAGATING. Cuttings taken early in the season before bud initiation.

COMMON PEST PROBLEMS. Aphids and whiteflies both love lantanas. (See Specific Pests and Diseases, page 42.)

Lavandula (lavender)
Most are hardy to at least 15°F (-9°C)

OVERWINTERING. Cool and bright (see page 24).

PROPAGATING. Cuttings.

COMMON PEST PROBLEMS. None.

Lotus (parrot's beak)
Hardy to at least 35°F (2°C)

OVERWINTERING. Cool and bright (see page 24) — in a greenhouse, our plants generally bloomed in midwinter, an exhilarating and cheery sight. To avoid eliminating blooms, do not prune back before overwintering.

PROPAGATING. Cuttings.

COMMON PEST PROBLEMS. None.

Lupinus albifrons (silver lupine)

Hardy to at least 25°F (-4°C)

OVERWINTERING. Cool and bright (see page 24). Allow soil to dry out very well between waterings. Do not prune if you want winter blooms.

PROPAGATING. Cuttings taken early in winter, before bud initiation.

COMMON PEST PROBLEMS. None.

Malvastrum lateritium (malvastrum)

Hardy to at least 25°F (-4°C)

OVERWINTERING. Cool and bright (see page 24). The habit of malvastrum is open and somewhat rangy — prune lightly to shape, but watch out for those flower buds!

PROPAGATING. Cuttings.

COMMON PEST PROBLEMS. Aphids seem to find most malvaceous plants delicious. (See Specific Pests and Diseases, page 42.)

Mandevilla (Chilean jasmine, mandevilla)

Hardy to at least 45°F (7°C)

OVERWINTERING. Cool and bright (see page 24); cool temperatures minimize insect infestations. Prune as necessary to keep the plant manageable.

PROPAGATING. Cultivars by cuttings; species by seed, although it may be a year or so before they bloom.

COMMON PEST PROBLEMS. Aphids, whiteflies. (See Specific Pests and Diseases, page 42.)

Manihot (cassava, manioc, tapioca)
Hardy to at least 45°F (7°C)

OVERWINTERING. Warm and sunny. If not kept warm enough, manihot may go dormant, but it will revive with increased light and warmth in spring. Keep it on the dry side all winter. You can let it go dormant and set it in a cooler, darker spot, like the basement, but in this case, make sure it doesn't ever dry out completely. Do not prune. (See Sunny & Warm, page 14, and Dark & Damp, page 29.)

PROPAGATING. Cuttings.

COMMON PEST PROBLEMS. None.

Manettia (firecracker vine, manettia)
Hardy to at least 45°F (7°C)

OVERWINTERING. Cool and bright (see page 24). This vigorous plant may benefit from a pruning now and then.

PROPAGATING. Easy to grow from seed.

COMMON PEST PROBLEMS. None.

Melianthus (honey flower, peanut butter plant)
Hardy to at least 35°F (2°C)

OVERWINTERING. Cool and bright (see page 24). Prune back hard in the fall.

PROPAGATING. Species are easily grown from seed. The cultivars are trickier and must be vegetatively propagated.

COMMON PEST PROBLEMS. None that we know of, although situating the plants in a location that is too windy or too sunny can result in damaged foliage. Placement in semi-shade is best in most North American gardens.

Musa (banana, plantain)

Hardiness varies

OVERWINTERING. Warm and sunny (see page 14); winter temperatures above 40°F (4°C). Many gardeners also have success overwintering dormant bananas in a dark basement; if using this method, be sure to keep the soil dry.

PROPAGATING. Division of pups. Because bananas are monocarpic, the parent plant dies after one full season. In cold climates, this may take more than one calendar year, but in our experience, once a banana has bloomed, the parent plant will not survive long.

COMMON PEST PROBLEMS. None.

Mussaenda (mussaenda)

Hardy to at least 45°F (7°C)

OVERWINTERING. Warm and sunny (see page 14). Prune to shape when necessary.

PROPAGATING. Cuttings.

COMMON PEST PROBLEMS. None.

Neoregelia (neoregelia)

Hardy to at least 45°F (7°C)

OVERWINTERING. Easy to keep as houseplants, they're reasonably happy without large amounts of sunshine. Neoregelias are especially appreciative of visits to the shower. In dry indoor heat, it's a good idea to keep the plant's central funnel filled with water. Occasional removal of old leaves is good, but otherwise, no pruning is necessary. (See Sunny & Warm, page 14.)

PROPAGATING. Division of offsets.

COMMON PEST PROBLEMS. None.

Nerium oleander (oleander, rose bay)

Hardy to at least 35°F (2°C)

OVERWINTERING. Cool and bright (see page 24).

PROPAGATING. Cuttings.

COMMON PEST PROBLEMS. None.

Ocimum basilicum (sweet basil)

Hardy to at least 45°F (7°C)

OVERWINTERING. Bright, but not too cool. Storage between 50 and 65°F (10–18°C) is best; warmer temperatures will encourage the growth of aphid populations. Water sparingly. Frequent pruning for culinary use and for shaping is an excellent idea. (See Cool & Bright, page 24.)

PROPAGATING. Cuttings.

COMMON PEST PROBLEMS. If this plant is kept too wet or does not receive adequate sunlight, botrytis, mildew, and damping-off are all possibilities.

Osmanthus fragrans (sweet olive)

Hardy to at least 35°F (2°C)

OVERWINTERING. Cool and bright (see page 24). Any pruning is best done after bloom, in the spring.

PROPAGATING. Cuttings.

COMMON PEST PROBLEMS. None.

Osteospermum (osteospermum)

Hardy to at least 35°F (2°C)

OVERWINTERING. Cool and bright (see page 24). As osteospermums bloom during the winter, refrain from pruning except for removal of spent blooms.

PROPAGATING. Species can be grown easily from seed. The hybrids should be propagated by cuttings.

COMMON PEST PROBLEMS. If osteospermums experience stressful conditions, aphids may find them attractive. (See Specific Pests and Diseases, page 42.)

Oxalis (oxalis, shamrock)

Hardiness varies

OVERWINTERING. Cool and bright (see page 24). Dormant types will require little active care. Those that continue to grow through the winter may benefit from a light shearing at some point.

PROPAGATING. This depends on the type. *Oxalis* species that have a dormant period are best propagated by repotting the corms. Other types can remain in containers and continue to grow even in the winter, given cool and relatively bright conditions. Propagate these species from cuttings.

COMMON PEST PROBLEMS. None.

Passiflora (passionflower)

Hardiness varies

OVERWINTERING. Cool and bright (see page 24). Passionflowers require good drainage and thrive on frequent feeding. Because they're vigorous growers, regular pruning will keep them looking their best.

PROPAGATING. Many of the species can be grown from seed, although this may be challenging. Collect fresh seed and soak it before sowing. Most passionflowers are easily rooted from tip cuttings taken in early spring.

COMMON PEST PROBLEMS. Whiteflies and spider mites may find these attractive. (See Specific Pests and Diseases, page 42.)

Pelargonium (geranium)

Hardy to at least 45°F (7°C)

OVERWINTERING. Cool and bright (see page 24). Water sparingly; remember that the South African winter is a dry one. Keep dead leaves picked off, and trim spent flower clusters as needed.

PROPAGATING. Cuttings.

COMMON PEST PROBLEMS. During the winter months, geraniums may be troubled by rust; discourage this problem by removing and disposing of infected leaves. Botrytis, which can also be a seasonal issue, will be similarly discouraged by the removal of spent blossoms and the prevalence of good air circulation.

Pentas (pentas, star cluster)
Hardy to at least 20°F (-7°C)

OVERWINTERING. Although pentas bloom and grow best in warm conditions, they will store well in a cool, bright location where they will become dormant. (See Sunny & Warm, page 14, and Cool & Bright, page 24.)

PROPAGATING. Cultivars must be propagated by cuttings.

COMMON PEST PROBLEMS. Aphids, whiteflies. (See Specific Pests and Diseases, page 42.)

Phormium (flax lily, New Zealand flax)
Hardy to at least 35°F (2°C)

OVERWINTERING. Although they benefit from a considerable amount of water when in active growth, we have found that the key to the successful overwintering of phormiums is to keep them dry in cool and bright conditions. Wet and cool conditions can stress them, predisposing them to winter demise. Phormiums should not be pruned; merely remove old leaves as needed. (See Cool & Bright, page 24.)

PROPAGATING. Species may be grown from seed, especially if your plant flowers and sets seed. The cultivars are generally produced by division. Newly divided plants will take some time to recover.

COMMON PEST PROBLEMS. Most problems we have encountered with phormiums stem from over-watering, not pests.

Phygelius (cape fuchsia, phygelius)
Hardy to at least 25°F (-4°C)

OVERWINTERING. Cool and bright (see page 24). Cut plants back hard in the fall and repeat as needed.

PROPAGATING. Cuttings.

COMMON PEST PROBLEMS. None.

Plectranthus (plectranthus)
Hardy to at least 35°F (2°C)

OVERWINTERING. Cool and bright (see page 24). Prune to shape as desired.

PROPAGATING. Species may be grown from seed. Cultivars are best grown from cuttings.

COMMON PEST PROBLEMS. None.

Plumbago (leadwort)
Hardy to at least 20°F (-7°C)

OVERWINTERING. Cool and bright (see page 24). Prune to shape in the fall.

PROPAGATING. Species may be grown from seed. Cultivars should be grown from cuttings.

COMMON PEST PROBLEMS. Both spider mites and whiteflies adore plumbago; be vigilant. (See Specific Pests and Diseases, page 42.)

Polianthes tuberosa (tuberose)
Hardy to at least 35°F (2°C)

OVERWINTERING. Cool and bright (see page 24).

PROPAGATING. The bulbs form offsets that are easily divided.

COMMON PEST PROBLEMS. None.

Punica granatum (pomegranate)
Hardy to at least 35°F (2°C)

OVERWINTERING. Cool and bright (see page 24). Prune to shape as desired.

PROPAGATING. Species are easily grown from seed, and cultivars should be propagated from cuttings.

COMMON PEST PROBLEMS. None.

Rhodochiton atrosanguineus (purple bell vine, rhodochiton)
Hardy to at least 25°F (-4°C)

OVERWINTERING. Cool and bright. It can also be placed in warmer and sunny conditions, but then it will stay in active growth. In either case, prune back fairly hard to reduce the size of the plant. (See Sunny & Warm, page 14, and Cool & Bright, page 24.)

PROPAGATING. Seeds.

COMMON PEST PROBLEMS. None.

Rosmarinus officinalis (rosemary)

Hardy to at least -5°F (-20°C)

OVERWINTERING. Cool and bright (see page 24) — the cooler and brighter, the better. Prune to shape.

PROPAGATING. Cuttings.

COMMON PEST PROBLEMS. Aphids. Powdery mildew is often a serious problem when overwintering rosemary indoors. The best preventives are good air circulation and cool growing conditions — temperatures between 30 and 40°F (-1–4°C) are ideal. It is also important not to over-water. (See Specific Pests and Diseases, page 42.)

Ruellia (Christmas pride, monkey plant, ruellia)

Hardiness varies from -25 to 30°F (-32 to -1°C)

OVERWINTERING. Cool and bright (see page 24). Do not be afraid to prune hard in the fall and when necessary thereafter.

PROPAGATING. Cuttings root rapidly. Species can be grown from seed.

COMMON PEST PROBLEMS. None.

Salvia (sage)

Hardiness varies

OVERWINTERING. Cool and bright, but some gardeners have successfully overwintered salvias in dark, dry conditions. It is worth experimenting with this if there are no other options. *Salvia patens* and *S. guaranitica* can be overwintered as a tuber, in dark and damp conditions. Most salvias should be cut back hard in the fall. (See Cool & Bright, page 24, and Dark & Dry, page 32.)

PROPAGATING. For the most part, the species grow easily from seed; cultivars and selections, from cuttings.

COMMON PEST PROBLEMS. In greenhouses, aphids are periodically a problem, but this is a good illustration of how a pest issue that is troublesome when plants are confined indoors will generally clear up quickly when the plants are moved outside. (See Specific Pests and Diseases, page 42.)

Senecio (natal ivy, orangeglow vine, senecio)
Hardiness varies

OVERWINTERING. Cool and bright (see page 24). Prune to shape as desired.

PROPAGATING. Cuttings.

COMMON PEST PROBLEMS. None.

Setaria palmifolia (palm grass)
Hardy to at least 35°F (2°C)

OVERWINTERING. Cool and bright (see page 24).

PROPAGATING. Division.

COMMON PEST PROBLEMS. Aphids. (See Specific Pests and Diseases, page 42.)

Sinningia (florist's gloxinia)
Hardy to at least 45°F (7°C)

OVERWINTERING. Dark and dry (see page 32). Sinningia's preference for dry winters makes it a trouble-free tender perennial to store. We have put the entire pot down in the cellar for the winter and brought it upstairs in the spring, at which point it revived abruptly with light and water. After exposure to a light frost, cut back sinningia stems before storing for the winter.

PROPAGATING. Most species are easily grown from seed and reach flowering size within a year. The mature plants form tubers, which you can separate when they are dormant. Even the florist's gloxinia is commonly potted up as a tuber in the spring or summer.

COMMON PEST PROBLEMS. Botrytis can become a problem if conditions are too moist.

Solanum (nightshade)
Hardiness varies by species

OVERWINTERING. Cool and bright (see page 24). Prune to shape as desired.

PROPAGATING. Species, seeds; cultivars, cuttings.

COMMON PEST PROBLEMS. Few pests want to mess with solanums.

Solenostemon scutellarioides (coleus)
Hardy to at least 45°F (7°C)

OVERWINTERING. Warm and sunny (see page 14), either as a whole plant or by cuttings. Particularly when grown indoors, coleus will require occasional pruning — do not be afraid to cut off quite a bit to make plants more manageable.

PROPAGATING. Cuttings.

COMMON PEST PROBLEMS. Aphids, scale, whiteflies. (See Specific Pests and Diseases, page 42.)

Strobilanthes (Persian shield, blue sage)
Hardiness varies by species

OVERWINTERING. Warm and sunny (see page 14). Cut back before moving plant inside.

PROPAGATING. Cuttings.

COMMON PEST PROBLEMS. None.

Thunbergia (black-eyed Susan vine, blue trumpet vine, sky vine, Bengal clock vine)
Hardy to at least 45°F (7°C)

OVERWINTERING. Individual species vary in their preferred temperature ranges; for instance, *Thunbergia alata* will thrive in bright, relatively cool environments, as low as 40°F (4°C); *T. mysorensis* will not. *T. grandiflora* grows vigorously in a range of conditions from sunny to shaded. It also likes cool temperatures, but is fine with considerable shade; *T. mysorensis* should be kept warm and sunny. Cut plants back hard before moving them indoors in the fall. (See Sunny & Warm, page 14, and Cool & Bright, page 24.)

PROPAGATING. Some species, such as *Thunbergia alata*, can be started from seed. Others may be easier to grow from cuttings.

COMMON PEST PROBLEMS. None.

Tibouchina (glory bush, purple glory tree)

Hardy to at least 45°F (7°C)

OVERWINTERING. Cool and bright is preferred, although warmer and sunny also works (see pages 24 and 14). Cut plants back hard in the fall before moving indoors.

PROPAGATING. Cuttings.

COMMON PEST PROBLEMS. None.

Trifolium (clover)

Hardy to at least 5°F (-15°C)

OVERWINTERING. Cool and bright (see page 24) really essential.

PROPAGATING. Cuttings.

COMMON PEST PROBLEMS. None.

Tweedia caerulea (southern star, tweedia)

Hardy to at least 35°F (2°C)

OVERWINTERING. Cool and bright (see page 24). Prune to shape as desired.

PROPAGATING. Just like its cousin *Asclepias syriaca*, the common roadside milkweed, pollinated *Tweedia caerulea* flowers turn into leathery pods full of silk-tasseled seeds; these germinate easily.

COMMON PEST PROBLEMS. Aphids. (See Specific Pests and Diseases, page 42.)

Uncinia (uncinia)
Hardy to at least 25°F (-4°C)

OVERWINTERING. Cool and bright (see page 24). Water sparingly. Remove old leaves, but do not trim.

PROPAGATING. Seeds.

COMMON PEST PROBLEMS. None.

Veltheimia (veltheimia)
Hardy to at least 35°F (2°C)

OVERWINTERING. Cool and bright for both species (see page 24). *Veltheimia capensis* will recuperate after bloom through the spring and much of the summer, and should be kept dry during this period. *V. bracteata* is in active growth all year.

PROPAGATING. Division of bulb offsets or by seed, if flowers are left to set them.

COMMON PEST PROBLEMS. None.

Xanthosoma (malanga, tannia, xanthosoma, yautia)
Hardy to at least 45°F (7°C)

OVERWINTERING. Warm, sunny, and humid. Trim off old leaves as the plant becomes dormant. Tubers can also be stored in dark and moist conditions, just like cannas. Keep the tuber cool but not cold — above 40°F (4°C). (See Sunny & Warm, page 14, and Dark & Damp, page 29.)

PROPAGATING. Division of offsets.

COMMON PEST PROBLEMS. The greatest challenge to cultivating these is providing adequate warmth and humidity. Otherwise, plants will sulk, leading to other complications, such as botrytis.

PLANTS THAT CAN BE PROPAGATED FROM CUTTINGS

Abutilon
Acalypha
Alonsoa
Aloysia
Alternanthera
Alyogyne
Amicia
Anagallis
Angelonia
Anisodontea
Arctotis
Argyranthemum
Aristolochia
Ballota
Begonia
Brachyglottis
Brugmansia
Ceratostigma
Cestrum
Citrus
Convolvulus
Coprosma
Cordyline
Cosmos
Cotyledon
Crassula
Cuphea
Diascia
Dichondra micrantha

Dicliptera suberecta
Erysimum
Eucomis
Felicia amelloides
Ficus carica
Fuchsia
Gardenia
Gynura auriantiaca
Haloragis erecta
Hamelia patens
Hebe
Heliotropium arborescens
Hibiscus
Iochroma
Ipomoea
Jasminum
Juanulloa mexicana
Kalanchoe
Kleinia
Lantana
Lavandula
Lotus
Lupinus albifrons
Malvastrum lateritum
Malvaviscus arboreus
Mandevilla
Manihot
Mussaenda
Myoporum

Nerium oleander
Nicotiana
Ocimum americanum
Origanum
Osamanthus fragrans
Osteospermum
Oxalis
Parahebe
Passiflora
Pelargonium
Pentas
Phygelius
Plecostachys serpyllifolia
Plectranthus
Plumbago
Punica granatum
Rosmarinus officinalis
Ruellia
Salvia
Senecio
Solanum
Solenostemon
  scutellarioides
Sollya heterophylla
Strobilanthes
Thunbergia
Tibouchina
Trifolium

TENDERS FOR CONTINUOUS BLOOM

Abutilon
Alonsoa
Anagallis
Anisodontea × hypomadara

Cestrum
Cuphea
Dicliptera suberecta
Plumbago

WINTER BLOOMERS

Abutilon
Alonsoa
Anisodontea × hypomadara
Argyranthemum
Ceratostigma wilmottianum
Cestrum
Convolvulus
Crassula
Cuphea
Dianella caerulea
Diascia

Dicliptera suberecta
Felicia amelloides
Heliotropium arborescens
Jasminum
Kalanchoe
Lotus
Lupinus albifrons
Malvastrum lateritium
Osmanthus fragrans
Plumbago
Veltheimia

PLANTS TO OVERWINTER IN A SUNNY AND WARM LOCATION

Acalypha
Agave
Aloe
Alternanthera
Aristolochia
Begonia
Colocasia
Crassula
Echeveria
Gasteria
Gynura auriantiaca
Haworthia
Hibiscus
Impatiens
Juanulloa mexicana

Kalanchoe
Kleinia
Lantana
Manihot
Musa
Mussaenda
Neoregelia
Pentas
Rhodochiton atrosanguineus
Solenostemon scutellariodes
Strobilanthes
Thunbergia
Tibouchina
Xanthosoma

PLANTS TO STORE DARK AND DAMP

Aloysia triphylla
Canna
Colocasia
Cosmos atrosanguineus
Dahlia

Ficus carica
Gunnera manicata
Ipomoea
Manihot
Xanthosoma

PLANTS TO STORE DARK AND DRY

Amorphophallus
Bessera elegans
Colocasia

Gladiolus
Salvia (some)
Sinningia

PLANTS TO OVERWINTER IN A COOL AND BRIGHT LOCATION

Abutilon
Agapanthus africanus
Agave
Aloe
Alonsoa
Aloysia triphylla
Alyogyne × amarcrinum
Amicia zygomeris
Anagallis
Angelonia angustifolia
Anigozanthos
Anisodontea × hypomadara
Arctotis × hybrida
Argyranthemum
Ballota
Begonia
Billardiera longiflora
Bouvardia
Brachyglottis
Brugmansia
Capsicum

Carex
Ceratostigma wilmottianum
Cestrum
Chondropetalum tectorum
Citrus
Convolvulus
Coprosma
Cordyline
Cotyledon
Crassula
Cuphea
Datura
Dianella caerulea
Diascia
Dichondra micrantha
Dicliptera suberecta
Echeveria
Erysimum
Eucomis
Felicia amelloides
Ficus carica

Fuchsia
Gardenia
Gasteria
Glaucium
Gunnera manicata
Haloragis erecta
Haworthia
Hebe
Heliotropium arborescens
Hibiscus
Iochroma
Ipomoea
Iresine herbstii
Jasminum
Juncus
Kalanchoe
Kniphofia
Lavandula
Lotus
Lupinus albifrons
Malvastrum lateritum
Malvaviscus arboreus
Mandevilla
Manettia
Melianthus
Myoporum
Nerium oleander
Ocimum americanum
Orthrosanthus chimboracensis

Osmanthus fragrans
Osteospermum
Oxalis
Parahebe
Passiflora
Pelargonium
Pentas
Phormium
Phygelius
Plectostachys serpyllifolia
Plectranthus
Plumbago
Polianthes tuberose
Punica granatum
Puya
Rhodochiton atrosanguineus
Rosmarinum officinalis
Ruellia
Salvia
Senecio
Setaria palmifolia
Solanum
Sollya heterophylla
Thunbergia
Tibouchina
Trifolium
Tweedia caerulea
Uncinia
Veltheimia

SOURCES FOR PLANTS AND SEEDS

Annie's Annuals & Perennials
888-266-4370
www.anniesannuals.com

Avant Gardens
508-998-8819
www.avantgardensne.com

Brent and Becky's Bulbs
877-661-2852
www.brentandbeckysbulbs.com

Chiltern Seeds Limited
+44-0-1491-824675
www.chilternseeds.co.uk

Digging Dog Nursery
707-937-1130
www.diggingdog.com

The Fragrant Path
sales@fragrantpathseeds.com
www.fragrantpathseeds.com

Glasshouse Works
740-662-2142
www.glasshouseworks.com

J. L. Hudson, Seedsman
inquiry@jlhudsonseeds.net
www.jlhudsonseeds.net

Jelitto Perennial Seeds
502-895-0807
www.jelitto.com

Kartuz Greenhouses
760-941-3613
www.kartuz.com

Logee's Greenhouses, Ltd.
888-330-8038
www.logees.com

Plant Delights Nursery, Inc.
919-772-4794
www.plantdelights.com

Plant World Seeds
+44-0-1803-872939
www.plant-world-seeds.com

Seedhunt.com
www.seedhunt.com

Thompson & Morgan
800-274-7333
www.thompson-morgan.com

INDEX